254

W9-AUK-720

BIKING TO THE ARCTIC CIRCLE

Adventures

With

Grandchildren

OTHER BOOKS BY ALLEN L. JOHNSON

Drive Through Russia? Impossible! - 1986

**Canoeing the Wabash -
Adventures With Grandchildren - 1991**

**Biking Across the Devil's Backbone -
Adventures With Grandchildren - 1997**

**Australia From the Back of a Camel
Adventures With Grandchildren - 1999**

Biking to the Arctic Circle

Adventures With Grandchildren

Allen L. Johnson

Creative Enterprises

Dayton, Ohio

PHOTO CREDIT

Pages 147,184. **Linda Chigi**
Page 14 . . . . **Jim Coppola**
Page 160. . . .. **Toby Curtis**
Page 31 . . . . **Elvin Isgrig**
Front & back covers, pages 104,145 . . . **Connie Johnson**
Page 58 . . . . **Karen Johnson**
Pages 168,178 . . . . **Karla Reichert**
Page 18 . . . . **Ann Stevens**
All other photos . . . . Author

FIRST EDITION

Published By Creative Enterprises
1040 Harvard Blvd.; Dayton, Ohio 45406-5047

Printed by Sheridan Books, Inc.
Chelsea, Michigan

Manufactured in the United States of America
ISBN: 1-880675-03-X

Library of Congress Catalog Card Number: 00-90359

iv

DEDICATION

This book is dedicated to my family for their help and understanding during my extended absence while accomplishing my adventures. The author also wishes to thank the following people for their editorial and proofreading assistance:

Nancy Carlson
Jim Coppola
Margaret Cotton
Gloria Johnson - chief editor and consultant
Karen Johnson
Karla Reichert
Linda Schwartz

CONTENTS

ILLUSTRATIONS

BIKING TO THE ARCTIC CIRCLE

Adventures

With

Grandchildren

CHAPTER 1

WHY DID I DO IT?

"Bike to the Arctic Circle? Impossible! There's ice and snow up there. It's only fit for polar bears and seals," one of my friends told me when he heard of my plan. Regardless, I did cycle to the Arctic Circle and I'd like to tell you why.

When most people retire, they dream of putting their feet up and relaxing. Not me. Since I retired from the Air Force in 1996 I've rollerbladed 400 miles around Holland; kayaked 40-foot-high tides in the Bay of Fundy; completed a 50 mile, one-day run along the Appalachian Trail; biked across the Canadian Maritime Provinces; ran three 26-mile marathons; completed a 210-mile, 2-day bike tour; driven a dogsled through the Boundary Waters area of Minnesota and competed in a triathlon. In the spring of 1999, I decided to pedal 4,000 miles from Dayton, Ohio to the Arctic Circle north of Fairbanks, Alaska.

Since I was a kid, I've wanted to travel up the Alaskan Highway and what better way to see it than by bicycle. My wife, Gloria, who accepts these adventures with a passive calm, opted to stay home where she managed the financial, communications and logistical end of the trip. The planned route was from Dayton across Indiana and Illinois to the Mississippi River at Savanna, Illinois; up the river to Minneapolis; across to Fargo, North Dakota; Minot and then to Portal on the Canadian border. From there, the route was through Regina and Saskatoon, Saskatchewan to Edmonton, Alberta; Dawson Creek, British Columbia; up the Alaskan Highway through Ft. Nelson and

Muncho Lake to Whitehorse, Yukon Territory. Then on to Tok, Alaska, Delta Junction, Fairbanks and finally up to the Arctic Circle.

I like to share my adventures with my grandchildren so I asked Paul (19 years old), Tracy (16 years old) and Kelsey (12 years old) if they would like to bike with me.

"No more working vacations," Tracy and Kelsey answered simultaneously. "We want to go somewhere tropical and lay on the beach."

"Can I bring my fishing pole?" Paul asked. "I wouldn't want to bike the entire distance, but I'd like to see the wilderness part."

If we could ride one hundred miles per day, six days a week we could complete the trip in two months. Since my grandchildren were unwilling to undertake the entire trip, I asked some friends if they would care to join me for part of the way?

My former co-worker, Jim Coppola, agreed to ride as far as Minneapolis. Karen Johnson, my niece from Boulder, Colorado, offered to ride a week across Southern Canada. Paul rode along the Alaskan Highway and Karla Reichert, my neighbor, decided to ride the last 600 miles through Alaska with me.

I already owned a good 21-speed road bicycle, Cannondale R-800, which I rode for the majority of the trip. To accommodate my riding companion, I bought another Cannondale R-800 in the spring. The skinny-tired road bikes are not suited for the numerous gravel stretches along the Alaskan Highway so I bought two 24-speed F-400 Cannondale mountain bikes with shock-absorber forks and shock seat posts. Riding for ten hours on bumpy gravel without some sort of a shock absorber can be very uncomfortable. We expected to have some mechanical problems with the bikes during the trip so we arranged with Whitman's Bike and Fitness stores in Dayton to ship replacement parts via overnight express when they were needed.

The prospect of carrying 50 pounds of camping and cooking equipment on the bicycle in addition to clothes, maps and tools didn't appeal to us. We opted to sleep in motels along the route. My riding companions breathed a sigh of relief at that decision. Using travel guides and the Internet "Phonebook," we made reservations at 46 motels between Dayton and Fairbanks a month before the trip. A daily destination limited our flexibility of stopping early on a bad biking day or going further on a good one. If we changed one reservation, it would throw our entire schedule out of whack. However, since rooms along the Alaskan Highway are severely limited, it was necessary to make reservations in advance to guarantee a room.

We didn't use a support vehicle on our previous 600-mile-long bike tour with granddaughter, Tracy, (Johnson, 1997). Originally, I planned to ride to Alaska without support. However, my more-cautious fellow riders suggested a support vehicle would be a good idea. Villages are spaced at 50 to 100 mile intervals along the Alaskan Highway with no facilities in-between. Our daughter-in-law, Connie Johnson, seemed like the logical person to drive a van across Canada and Alaska supporting us.

"I'd love to," Connie said. "I've always wanted to see Alaska!"

We rented a mini-van from Hertz at Edmonton, Alberta, and Connie drove it one-way to Anchorage, Alaska. With the van we could carry food, water and ice, making us less dependent on the widely spaced gas stations and grocery stores in the Yukon. The van helped solve the complicated problem of how to transport the various bicycles to the places they were needed. We used five different bikes during the trip. I used my road bike most of the way to Alaska. Jim rode his own bike from Dayton to Minneapolis and took it home on the bus. Gloria shipped the second road bike United Parcel Service to Regina for Karen to ride. She rode it to Edmonton, Paul rode it to Whitehorse and Karla rode it to Fairbanks. Gloria also shipped two mountain bikes to Edmonton since we picked the van up there. Having the van allowed us to carry whichever bikes we weren't riding. Paul, Karla and I switched to the mountain bikes for part of the Alaskan Highway and for the last 200 miles up the gravel road to the Arctic Circle.

Early May was chosen for our departure date based on the expected weather. April in Ohio can still be cold, and if we waited until June we could expect some very hot days before finishing the ride in August. By starting in May we could expect cool weather most of the way since spring comes to Alaska and the Yukon in June.

"How can we help out?" several friends asked.

"How about pledging a contribution related to the mileage?" I suggested. "It'll give us more incentive to ride the whole distance. The money will go directly to the Salvation Army." About 100 friends, relatives and acquaintances pledged a penny a mile.

Planning and preparation took most of a year. There was also six months of intensive physical conditioning including running, biking and swimming. The final three months included mapping out the route (Appendix 1), confirming motel reservations (Appendix 2), assembling a pack (Appendix 3) and getting mentally ready to set off for Alaska.

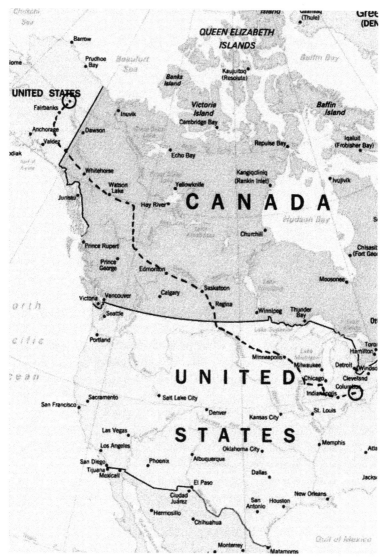

Bike Route From Dayton to the Arctic Circle

CHAPTER 2

GOOD LUCK AND GOD'S SPEED

What have we forgotten to pack? What have we overlooked? This would be the most physically challenging adventure of our lives. I packed route maps, the computer, bike tools, spare tubes, a toothbrush, underwear, socks and a rain jacket. If we forgot anything, we would buy it along the way or have Gloria send it to us.

To generate some publicity for the Salvation Army pledges, I talked with newspaper columnist, Dale Huffman. He wrote a nice article, with photos, about the planned trip in the Dayton Daily News on May 3, 1999 that caught the attention of the Associated Press and local TV stations.

On May 5, 1999, Jim and I got up at 5:00 a.m. We loaded all our bags on the bikes for the first time and went for a quick ride down Broadway Street to check out the handling of the fully loaded bikes. Karla, Mary and Carl Reichert showed up along with neighbors, Mr. Hall, Rose and Don Peacock, the Channel 2 and Channel 22 news people and Bruce Wooly from Whitman's bike shop. After a final round of photos, good-byes, hugs and handshakes, Jim, Bruce and I biked up Harvard Boulevard to shouts of "Good luck and God's speed." The Arctic bike trip was officially underway! The TV crews went ahead and filmed us as we pedaled out of town. A light rain fell as we rode west from Dayton at about 15 miles per hour (mph). It felt good to finally be underway.

We made our first rest stop at Hardee's Restaurant in Eaton, Ohio, for a cinnamon bun and a glass of milk. The waitress there was impressed with our undertaking.

"I'd like to buy you each a hot apple pie so you'll have enough energy to make it through Indiana," she said.

We accepted.

Jim fixing 2nd flat tire on the first day

"My tire is flat," Jim said as we walked out of Hardee's. One hour into our two-month trip and already we had a problem. Jim and Bruce fixed the tire while I tried without success to locate the cause for the leak.   Jim used his high-tech, compressed-air bottle to pump the tire up. Ten minutes down the road, Jim's tire went flat again.

"Twenty-five miles and two flats. At this rate, we can expect 320 flats over the 4,000-mile trip," I calculated.

We looked carefully at the punctured tube and finally determined that the high tire pressure, 100 pounds, was forcing the tube into small holes in the rim. The solution? Duct tape, a new tube and less pressure.

At Richmond, Indiana, Bruce left Jim and me.

"Wish I had time to go all the way with you, but I still have to earn a living," Bruce said as he headed back to Dayton.

The weather became warm and sunny as Jim and I pedaled out of Richmond. An hour later, as I swerved to avoid a stick in the road, my saddlebag swung into the rear tire and my bike came to a screeching stop.

"You broke a spoke and bent the rim," Jim said as he helped extract the saddlebag from the wheel. The rear rim was bent so badly, the wheel wouldn't rotate.

"Shall we call Whitman's to bring a new wheel over?" I asked.

"Naw," Jim said. "If you've got a spoke wrench, I think I can straighten your rim enough so you can still ride."

I handed Jim the wrench. He tightened the spokes on one side and loosened those on the other side.

"There," he said as he spun the wheel. "That should get you to Noblesville."

I mounted up and started down the road. There was a slight wobble in my rear wheel, but I could still ride at 15 mph.

"For Crying Out Loud" the 30-foot long sign outside of Hagerstown declared. A life-sized, open-mouth hippopotamus stood next to the sign. It turned out to be an advertisement for an auctioneer who owned the corner lot.

"Bang," the tube in my rear tire exploded as I bounced over a rough railroad track at the edge of New Castle. I had just aired up my tires minutes before to 100-pounds pressure to reduce their road resistance. The rim liner had slipped and the increased air pressure forced the tube down one of the spoke holes. After realigning the rim liner and putting the new tube in, I pumped the tire up to 60-pounds pressure. Was our adventure doomed? We hadn't completed the first day of our two-month trip and already we had three flat tires and a broken spoke.

Twelve hours and 109 miles from our cheerful start we pedaled into the Frederick-Talbott Inn in Noblesville tired, bedraggled and a bit discouraged.

"Is there any place to get a bike wheel fixed near here?" I asked Susan, the owner of the Inn.

8

"I drive right by a bike shop on my way home," Susan said. "I'm leaving in a few minutes and I'd be glad to drop the wheel off there for you."

Jim and I each took a long, steaming-hot shower to soak the road dirt and weariness off us. I felt much better after that.

Ann Price-Perkins, my high school classmate who lived in nearby Indianapolis, picked us up and "drove" us to a first-class restaurant for supper. It felt good not to have to pedal to supper. After a delightful meal and a chance to catch up on old-times, Ann drove us to the Bike Outfitter on Allisonville Road to pick up my bike wheel. The bike technician, James Zenor, did an excellent job of aligning the bent rim. It didn't wobble. He threw in an extra spoke in the unlikely event that I broke another one.

We had a restful night's sleep and Susan cooked us a delicious breakfast of French toast, eggs, bacon and fruit. We were ready to tackle the world again! A radio station in Terre Haute called while we were eating breakfast and did an on-the-air interview. They had seen the Associated Press news release and contacted Gloria to get our telephone number.

We left Noblesville in a light rain and pedaled northwest on Route 38. Our first rest stop was at a gas station in Sheridan, Indiana.

"You're biking to Alaska?" the blond waitress asked. "Why?"

"I like to have adventures with my grandchildren," I explained. "I've taken my grandson on a 500-mile canoe trip down the Wabash, my granddaughter on a 600-mile bike trip across the Mid-West and my older grandchildren on a 140-mile camel safari across the Australian Outback. This year, I decided to fulfill my childhood dream of seeing the Alaskan Highway. What better way to see it than by bike?"

The local sheriff, who was drinking coffee at the next booth, came over to ask us about our trip.

9

"I've got an RV and we drive all over the country on two-lane roads to see the sights. In three years when I retire, we're going to drive to Alaska," he said. "I hear the Alaskan Highway gets pretty bad in spots."

"I talked to a fellow from Whitehorse, Yukon last week and he said the highway is in pretty good shape now. It's mostly smooth asphalt, but about ten percent of it is still gravel and under reconstruction," I said. "I'm anxious to see what the Yukon looks like."

Big, black, threatening clouds rolled in accompanied by gale-force winds, dumping buckets of water on Sheridan. After the rain eased off, we started on our way. We were lucky not to be caught between towns when the storm hit. God was watching over us.

A strong head wind picked up after the storm, blowing at 15 to 20 mph. I struggled to make 8 mph against the wind. At Frankfort we stopped at the local IGA deli and bought a freshly made chicken-salad sandwich for lunch.

As we pedaled west into the head wind, I had trouble keeping pace with Jim. I kept falling further and further behind.

"Come up alongside and draft off me," Jim offered, noticing my plight.

I accepted willingly, pulling my front wheel up close to Jim's rear wheel so I could take advantage of the partial vacuum Jim's bike created. Drafting improved my speed from an 8-mph pace to 10 mph, enough to knock one or two hours off the day's riding time.

On State Route 28 between Odell and Attica we passed a beautiful 130-year-old brick manor house with a sign out front-- "Bonnie's Bygones, Antiques for Sale."

Bonnie and Don Opperman bought the house 25 years ago and restored it to its original elegance. "The house was built in 1870 by the Odells, a wealthy family from Brown County Ohio," Bonnie told us. "They farmed 400 acres of very rich land. When we bought the house it was in bad shape. The soffits were rotten out and there were 500 pigeons living in the attic. There was a lot of water damage and just rough wear."

Bonnie gave us a tour of the house. The downstairs consists of a kitchen, dining room, parlor, sitting room and library. From the front hall a free-hanging spiral staircase leads to the second floor. The wall by the staircase curves with the stairs and has niches built into the corners to set flower vases. The main bedrooms are off the upstairs hall with a nursery in the back. The nursery also had a door leading to the back stairs and the servant's quarters. Bonnie displayed antique toys, dolls, doll quilts and doll furniture in the servant's quarters. The whole house is furnished in early American or pioneer style. The kitchen still has an icebox and the blue enameled cast-iron cooking stove has been converted to electric by the addition of a plate holding an electric stovetop.

"We can convert it back to its original condition by lifting the stove-top out and placing the old cast-iron top back in place," Bonnie's husband, Don, told us.

"How long have you been selling antiques?" I asked.

"About 30 years," Bonnie said. "I thought this house would make the perfect setting for the business. We specialized in country furniture, but furniture is becoming hard to find so now I sell mostly small primitives, stoneware, pottery, glassware, toys and a bit of furniture."

"Does this old house have a ghost?" I asked.

"No, we've never seen a ghost, but we do have a witch," Bonnie said with a chuckle. "Every Halloween I put a witch out in front of the house."

Ominous big, black clouds filled the sky as the sun sunk low in the west. Holes appeared in the clouds, sending golden shafts of light down to the ground. It was interesting to watch the shaft move around like search lights as the clouds moved, pointing first to the left, then straight down and then to the right as though God was picking out specific people or places to send his personal message.

It was almost dark when we pedaled into Attica and arrived at the beautiful Apple Inn. Carolyn Carlson has decorated this lovely old house with her grandmother's antiques. It felt like I was walking into a comfortable museum as she and her brother, Don, welcomed us.

"We're cooking some bluegills for supper," Don said. "Would you like to join us?"

Bluegills are my favorite fish, and I ate my fill of the freshly caught pan fish. Don soaked them in a beer and egg batter before pan frying them, giving the fish a delicious smell and a delicate taste. Jim went back for seconds and thirds as well.

Friends of Carolyn ate supper with us. After I described the bike trip and my dream of seeing the Alaskan Highway, John related his dream of sailing down the inland waterway along the East Coast to Florida.

"We have a 35-foot sailboat and we head south in the winter. Sometimes we stay on the East Coast of Florida and sometimes we sail around to Fort Myers," John explained. "Always wanted to sail."

It seems that many people have dreams; me, John, the sheriff, the gas station attendant. It is amazing how many people pursue their dreams. We hear about all the couch potatoes who spend their time living other people's dreams on TV, but there are a lot of people who grab the brass ring and live life to the fullest.

After supper, Jim and I relaxed in the Apple Inn's hot tub. Special jets massaged our sore neck muscles, different ones for our backs, our thighs and even our feet. Oh, how those hot water jets soothed our weary muscles. We fought the wind for ten and a half-hours to cover 83 miles and our muscles were complaining.

Walking down the stairs in the morning made me realize that my thighs were not used to pedaling 100 miles day after day. Oh, that hurt! However, a fantastic breakfast of silver-dollar

12

blueberry pancakes, eggs, pork cutlet and grapefruit put me in a great mood--until I walked out to my bike and noticed my front tire was flat. Four flats in two days! I was not in a very good mood as I changed the tube. To make matters worse, the new tube went flat before I could pedal out of the driveway. Five flats! The problem was a bad repair on the tube that had the blowout the day before. I installed a new tube and cautiously Jim and I pedaled away from the Apple Inn. We crossed the historic Wabash River that grandson Paul and I canoed down nine years before, (Johnson, 1991) and pedaled up a big hill out of Attica.

Climbing that hill was a good way to get my heart started in the morning. Four miles later we stopped in Williamsport to view the highest waterfalls in Indiana--90 feet high. A good-sized stream of water was crashing over the falls, thanks to an overnight rain. As we rode west on Route 28, the gentle morning breeze blossomed into a stiff gale--20-mph wind with gusts to 35 mph. The eddy from a passing truck caused us to weave all over the highway. One big gust blew me completely off the road and into the ditch. At that point, Jim and I decided to walk the bikes for a ways. Pedaling as hard as we could, we were only making 6 mph riding against the wind and we could walk at 4 mph with a lot less effort.

"This is not what long-distance pleasure biking is supposed to be like," I said.

"No, but this is real life," Jim responded with a grin.

We walked our bikes for 15 or 20 minutes and then hopped back on and I resumed drafting behind Jim. Our speed averaged 8 to 10 mph against the wind, but picked up to 15 mph whenever we encountered a tree-lined windbreak. Unfortunately, farmers are not in the business of planting trees so that wasn't very often. Three hours out of Attica, we crossed the Indiana state line into Illinois. Time for a rest stop and a photo of the "Welcome to Illinois" sign.

13

The third day we crossed from Indiana into Illinois

After fighting the wind for another two hours, we finally reached Route 49, turned north and flew with the wind at our backs--20 to 22 mph. That immediately brightened our sagging spirits. At Cissna Park, we stopped in a churchyard to rest and both fell asleep for about 20 minutes lying under an oak tree. Tired? Not us!

An hour later, we pedaled toward Kankakee where we had arranged for my cousin's husband, Bob McCoy, to meet us with his truck. The plan was to spend the night at Pat and Bob's farmhouse near Joliet, Illinois, and have Bob drive us back to our stopping point in the morning. With eight and a half-hours of hard pedaling, we covered 83 miles on Friday. That evening we enjoyed a great meal and caught up on family happenings while warming our feet in front of a roaring wood fire. Life is good!

Dayna, her son Jared and owner Jan Richmond waited on us

On Saturday morning Bob dropped us off, and we flew along the road with the wind at our back, going over 30 mph down some of the hills. Even with rest stops, our average speed was a respectable 15 mph on our way to Troy Grove, Illinois. At lunch time we stopped at the Serena Café along scenic Route 52 in Serena, Illinois. The café was a 25-foot square, one-story building characteristic of a 1940s, small town diner where everyone knew each other. Inside, there were six or eight tables and a 20-foot long counter with stools. Jim and I chose the counter. Personal coffee cups hung on the wall for each regular customer. If one of the retired customers didn't show up at their regular time, someone in the cafe would call and check if they were all right.

I felt so comfortable walking into the café, as if I'd been coming there all my life. Everyone in the café spoke to us. Dayna, the waitress, asked Jim where we were headed.

"Alaska."

That got her attention. She asked how, why and how long would it take us. Whenever someone else came in, Dayna mentioned our planned destination. We ordered a sandwich and a cinnamon bun. I have never seen a cinnamon bun that big! It filled a dinner plate and looked more like a cinnamon cake than a bun. Its fresh-baked aroma filled the café with a pleasant bakery smell. I took photos of Dayna and the owner/cook, Jan Richmond, to document my story of the trip. We were treated like regular customers.

When we reached Troy Grove, Bob picked us up and drove back to his farmhouse where we enjoyed our first day off. On Sunday we attended church where I visited with Viola Leifheit, my 80-year-old cousin. The congregation said a special bike–trip prayer for us. We needed all the help we could get. The minister and his wife had taken a trip up the Alaskan Highway a few years before and the minister's wife regretted they didn't get to the Arctic Circle.

"I wanted to go, but my husband didn't think it was a good idea to drive up that rough gravel road to the Circle," she said.

The rest of Sunday we wrote in our journals, oiled the bikes and relaxed. It was a good first week of biking, covering 350 miles in 4 days.

CHAPTER 3

BIKING ALONG THE BEAUTIFUL MISSISSIPPI

The fastest gun in the west and famous marshal of Abilene, Wild Bill Hickok, was born in Troy Grove, Illinois, our Monday morning starting point. James Butler "Wild Bill" Hickok lived in Troy Grove from his birth in 1837 until he was 18. He was fascinated with guns since his youth. Instead of working his father's farm, he could usually be found roaming the nearby woods, honing his shooting skills by hunting wolves for bounty and providing fresh meat for his family. He roamed around the west until the Civil War and then worked for the Union Army as scout, spy and sharpshooter. Wild Bill always carried two ivory-handled Colt revolvers tucked in a red sash around his waist. He moved with cat-like grace, had lightning reflexes and shot with great accuracy using either hand.

While I admired Wild Bill Hickok, the special interest for me in Troy Grove was a visit with Nancy Carlisle Leopold, a childhood girlfriend, who currently lives in Troy Grove with her husband, Hank. Bob drove Jim and me to Nancy's house where we stopped for a cup of tea and an opportunity to brag about our respective grandchildren. Nancy had me outnumbered, 15 to 5.

"Where did Wild Bill live?" I asked.

"The family home was in the center of town one block south of Route 52, at the edge of the park. They say he used to hunt right down there along the Little Vermilion River," Nancy said, pointing out her window to a stand of trees a mile away. "The state put up a granite monument in the park and last year they added a carved wooden bust of Wild Bill. Would you like to see the church that Wild Bill's father help establish?"

"Sure."

Nancy and Hank drove us down to the park to see Wild Bill's bust and then to the nearby church. The handsome white

17

At Troy Grove we visited my friends Nancy and Hank

church sits on the corner across from the cemetery. It has recently been reroofed and sided so it doesn't look like a 150-year-old building.

"What's the current size of the congregation?" I asked.

"It's about 110 people," Hank said. "We think that's pretty big, considering the total population of Troy Grove is only 300. A lot of people from Mendota attend our church."

"Do any of Wild Bill's relatives still live here?" I asked.

"His great niece, Edith Hamon, lives up the road in Mendota," Nancy said. "She's in her 80s, but she still gets riled up when someone writes some wild tale about her great uncle."

One of the exciting aspects of the trip was that once I left Nancy's house I was on virgin roads. For the next 3,700 miles I had never seen the road I'd be biking on. Every curve would offer a brand new vista, every town a brand new opportunity to get lost. I love taking new roads and discovering new things.

For a boy who was 16-years-old before he ever ventured out of his small Southern Illinois hometown, the next 45 days promised to be the ultimate adventure.

From Troy Grove, Jim and I biked north to Dixon and stopped by Ronald Reagan's childhood home. As we were taking pictures of the house, Bill Jones, a local biker, walked over to find out where we were going.

"Alaska! That's great. I rode the Great Ohio Bike Adventure last year," he said, pointing to the GOBA shirt he was wearing. "Usually get in about 5,000 miles a year." He took our picture standing in front of Reagan's statue.

A little past Dixon, Jim's rear tire went flat. That made our sixth flat and we hadn't made it through a single day without at least one tube change. We stopped under the shade of a big maple tree in a farmyard and put a new tube in the tire. Jim and I were getting very proficient at changing tires. That one only took 12 minutes from start to finish. It appeared to be caused by a rock bruise or rim puncture so we put more duct tape inside the rim to hopefully avoid future problems.

The flashing red light of a police car caught my attention as it pulled alongside me at the outskirts of Savanna, Illinois.

"You need to ride on the edge of the road, not in the through-lane," the policeman told me through the open window of his car.

Jim and I were reluctant to ride on the edge of the turn lane because then we had to cross the turn-lane traffic at every intersection in order to continue straight, but after his emphatic warning we reluctantly moved over to the edge of the road.

We checked into the Radke Hotel in Savanna, Illinois, right on the Mississippi River. Our room was on the third floor of the old hotel and there was no elevator so the manager let us keep our bikes in the lobby overnight. We had to go through a maze of halls and stairs to get to our room. I felt like leaving a trail of breadcrumbs so I could find my way out in the morning. Our suite consisted of a large living room, a small bedroom and a bath. The railroad used to change crews in Savanna and the trainmen lived in these suites until the next train arrived.

Savanna "The Sportsman's Paradise," is a small, clean river town that is struggling to stay alive. Settled 170 years ago to support the steamboat and lumber businesses along the Mississippi, the town's economy became dependent on the nearby Savanna Army Depot during the 1900s. When it closed in the early 1990s, the tourist trade took over as the major employer and revenue generator. Excellent fishing, boating, hunting and camping facilities brings sportsmen from Chicago and all over Illinois. Savanna's main shopping district stretches along the Mississippi River with the residential area extending up the bluffs. Big, beautiful houses built by the successful riverboat captains stand on the highest hills overlooking the town and the river.

Our hotel room overlooked Main Street that was full of activity in the evening with shoppers, walkers, skateboarders and teenagers gossiping in small groups. Across the street was a biker's bar. The throaty roar of Harley Davidsons and the quiet purr of Hondas and Kawasakis riding into town broke the otherwise tranquil quiet of Savanna's Main Street.

For supper we walked to the Upper Deck where I ordered a pork tenderloin sandwich and salad. The tenderloin turned out to be a tasty eight-inch diameter piece of meat in a four-inch diameter bun. I love the good service and great food available at these small-town, family-run restaurants.

We biked up the Great River Road along the scenic Mississippi River on Tuesday morning with bald eagles, red-tailed hawks, blue herons and turkey vultures soaring overhead. The terrain was heavily wooded and basically flat. Jim and I raced the tugboats pushing barges of coal, gravel and oil up river. It wasn't hard to catch and pass the barges since they were only making 5 mph. We were cruising along at 15 mph.

Jim and I were talking about the sorry state of the world and ways to solve all the problems as we pedaled up a busy

20

intersection with Route 20. When I came to a stop at the hilly intersection, my shoe-clips wouldn't come unclipped from the pedals. In slow motion, the bike and I fell over in the gravel by the side of the road much like Arty Johnson used to do in his tricycle skit on "Laugh-In" back in the 1960s! So much for my grace and good form.

There were thousands of ducks in pens as we pedaled through Hanover, Illinois, the self-proclaimed "Mallard Capital of the World." I wonder how a town gets into the duck business? Was there a long-range plan or did the town-folk wake up one morning, look out the window and say, "Gosh, there are an awful lot of ducks walking around town. Let's corner the market on mallards."

Biking into Galena, Illinois, we stopped at a corner antique shop to ask directions to General Grant's house.

"It's one block down this road," the lady said, pointing to the side road. "How far are you biking?"

"We're headed to Alaska," I replied.

"Alaska! That's quite a ride from here. I lived in Alaska for 13 years. What part of Alaska are you going to?"

"Up the Dalton Highway to the Arctic Circle."

"That's a coincidence; I lived on the Dalton Highway when I was there," the lady said.

"Is there any place to stay in Livengood? I couldn't find any motels listed north of Fairbanks," I said.

"Nancy and Joe Carlson live just outside of Livengood, about 60 miles north of Fairbanks. I'm sure they'd be happy to put you up."

"Do you have their phone number?"

"They don't have a phone. As a matter of fact, they don't even have electricity. The best way to contact them is through 'Trapline Chatter.' Radio station KJNP at North Pole, Alaska, has a program called 'Trapline Chatter' on Saturday morning where they send out personal messages to the people who live on remote homesteads around Alaska. If you call the radio station and leave a message, Joe and Nancy will get a reply back to you. Tell Joe that Diane Dahlby suggested you contact them."

I am amazed at the many happy coincidences that occurred on this bike trip. We found a bike shop four miles from our motel in Noblesville Indiana that was open late in the evening and could repair the broken spoke and bent rim on my bike. Now, we ran into the one person out of 270 million people in the lower 48 states who previously lived on the Dalton Highway and could give us information about accommodations there. There is no doubt in my mind that these "coincidences" are God's answer to the prayers of dozens of our friends and relatives who were concerned about our progress and safety.

After thanking Diane, Jim and I biked down to General Grant's house and took a tour. It is a beautiful brick home decorated in 1850s-period furniture and staffed by a group of knowledgeable volunteers. One of the most interesting parts of the house is the kitchen. It is full of apple peelers, mechanical cherry pitters, butter churns, milk separators and other laborsaving devices for the busy kitchen staff. There is even a spring-driven spit for turning the meat roasting over the fireplace. The volunteers invited me to come back for the annual Grant family reunion held each summer. My mother was a Grant from Scotland and I believe we are distant relatives of General Grant.

As we rode out of Galena we passed a series of Classic Burma Shave signs.

They want 500 bucks
for a pedal bike!
Why, that's more
Than it cost
For my brand-new
Model T,
Grandpa wailed.
Burma Shave

There were some huge hills between Galena, Illinois and Plattsville, Wisconsin that would make San Francisco look flat. My thighs complained as I huffed and puffed up the grade. Crossing the Wisconsin border, we stopped for the traditional "Welcome to Wisconsin" photo opportunity. Seven beautiful, coal-black horses galloped over to the fence to welcome us. Interestingly, each horse had a white spot or star on its forehead.

We encountered several prominent billboards advertising real estate for sale from The Old Territory Land Company. They have a very catchy phone number, 777-1776. A number like that is easy to remember and worth its weight in advertising potential.

By the time Jim and I reached Lancaster, Wisconsin, we were hot and tired. At the edge of Lancaster stood an A&W Root Beer Stand complete with pretty carhops and frosty glass mugs of A&W root beer. Oh, did that ice-cold root beer taste good! It has been 40 years since I had a frosty mug of A&W root beer.

POW, flap, flap, flap. My rear tire went flat as I zoomed down a steep hill on the outskirts of Prairie du Chein. Cause? I'd hit a sharp rock in the road and it pinched the tube against the rim. This was very discouraging as it was my third flat of the day and occurred just two miles from our motel. Jim helped me change the tire by a field full of horses.

When we walked into the Holiday Motel to register, the clerk was holding the phone and asked if either of us was Mr. Johnson?

"You have a phone call," the clerk said, handing me the phone.

It was Norb Aschom from radio station WPRE in Prairie du Chein. He recorded a radio interview about the bike trip before we left Dayton and wanted an update. The update took about 20 minutes as I described our progress to date, problems and pleasures.

23

After the interview, I went to our room where Jim was busy checking and oiling his bike. My priority was a hot soak in the bathtub.

On Wednesday we continued along the Great River Road riding in a light, cold rain. Mid-morning my front tire blew out--another rim problem. There was a quarter-inch hole in the tube and another quarter-inch bulge about to blow. I took the tire off, wrapped the inside of the rim with duct tape, put a new tube in and pumped the tire back up. On the outskirts of Dakota, we stopped at a Quik-Stop to warm up and eat a snack. I asked for a cup of tea, but they didn't have any tea bags so I poured a cup of hot water and drank it.

"Nobody in Dakota ever asks for tea," the attendant told me.

A little past Dakota we stopped at dam/lock number nine to watch the barges locking through at Lynxville, "Where the River Rests." The tug and barges were too long for the lock. The deck hands tied the barges to one side of the lock and then unhooked the tug and motored up alongside the barges as the lock operator closed the downstream lock doors. After the operator raised the water and opened the upstream lock doors, the tug motored out and pulled the barges out of the lock. The tug unhooked again, went around behind the barges, hooked back up and started pushing the barges up-river again. The whole process took over 30 minutes.

A little after noon we pedaled into LaCross, Wisconsin, and then across the Mississippi River bridge into La Crescent, "The Apple Capital of Minnesota." The bridge floor was a grid made of metal strips set on their narrow edge. I had terrible visions of my skinny bike tires getting stuck in the grid or getting punctured on metal knobs sticking up. They didn't. We stopped at the Minnesota border for a "Welcome to Minnesota" photo with Governor Jessie Ventura and his feather boa in the background. Then we pedaled up the Minnesota side of the

Mississippi. It was a beautiful ride with big, tree-covered bluffs, lots of wild life and beautiful homes overlooking the river.

It started raining hard in the early afternoon, prompting us to pull rain ponchos out of our packs and put them on. My chest stayed dry, but my shoes and bike shorts got wet. Jim and I were both soaking wet and cold when we finally arrived at the Winona Days Inn. Jim asked the desk clerk where to find a laundry to dry our wet clothes. The desk clerk suggested a laundromat a couple of miles away. Not wanting to go back out in the cold rain, Jim sweet-talked the maid into letting us use the motel's industrial dryer. He stayed in the laundry room and helped her fold towels while our clothes dried.

For supper we walked next door to a family restaurant. I ordered potato soup, salad, chicken stir-fry, cherry pie and ice cream---I was starving. Since I started riding, my appetite has increased every day. I drank two glasses of water and three glasses of iced tea with supper.

I called home every night from the motel to report our progress to Gloria. She handled our logistics, sent us care packages, mailed the mountain bikes to Canada and kept our friends up to date on our progress. She was a little short with me the night before because she'd missed her afternoon nap three days in a row due to all the bike trip activities. By Wednesday evening, she was in a better mood. Things slowed down and she was able to take her nap.

A cold rain was still falling Thursday morning as we left Winona. Our route took us through Wabasha, Minnesota, whose claim to fame is that the movie, "Grumpy Old Men" with Jack Lemon and Walter Mathau was filmed there. Besides the old movie sets, it is possible to visit "Slippery's Bar" which was featured in the movie. We didn't.

Mid-morning we stopped for lunch at a Subway sandwich shop in Lake City, "where water skiing originated." Two ladies who were also eating in Subways asked where we were headed.

"Alaska," Jim said and the ladies asked some more questions. I gave them one of the bike trip information handouts and they read about the Salvation Army penny-a-mile pledge.

"Can we pledge?" they asked.

"Sure, just send your pledge to the Salvation Army address in the write-up."

We passed through Red Wing, Minnesota, the home of the Red Wing Shoe and Boot Company. I had a pair of Red Wing boots when I was a kid. They were my favorite boots of all time.

At Hastings, Minnesota, we stopped to photograph a beautiful, well-preserved brownstone mansion built in 1863 by a local millionaire, LeDuc Simmons.

From Hastings we rode up and down a series of corrugated hills, arriving at Lake Elmo, a suburb of Minneapolis, about 5:00 p.m. My friends, Mike and Barb Miller, who live in Lake Elmo, agreed to put us up for the night.

"This was the first day of the ride that we did not have a flat tire," I told Mike as we sat around their kitchen table.

"I heard a bang in the garage and saw your back tire go flat," Jim said as he walked in the kitchen.

I thought he was joking, but when I checked I found the tube had ruptured on the rim spoke hole. I duck taped the rear rim to prevent any further problems.

Jim had to go back to work in Washington, DC. After supper, Mike drove him to the Greyhound station and put him and his bike on the bus. I spent a relaxed evening catching up on what the Millers have been doing and the adventures of their grandchildren. They have a beautiful cat named Bob that rubbed against my legs repeatedly.

"What kind of cat is Bob?" I asked. "He looks like a Russian Blue or Burmese."

"He's a Minnesota stray," Mike explained. "We got him at the pound."

CHAPTER 4

RIDING SOLO TO FARGO

Friday morning I was up before the Millers so I sat at the kitchen table and typed up my daily journal. Bob wove between my legs, then walked over to his dish and gave that "feed me" look. I didn't know where his cat food was so I ignored him. He became very impatient after trying eight or nine times to get me to feed him. Finally, Barb came in the kitchen and fed him.

I couldn't figure out a safe bike route through downtown Minneapolis, even with Mike's help. City traffic is terrible! The total mileage from Dayton to the Arctic Circle is 4,180. I've advertised the trip as a 4,000-mile bike ride so I had 180 miles extra that I could take as a "gimmee," a golf putt your opponent gives you credit for without you putting or in my case a free ride. Getting across Minneapolis was a very necessary gimmee. I put my bike on the back of Mike's car and he and Barb drove me across town. Once through the heavy traffic, Mike stopped in a strip mall; I took my bike off the car and loaded my bags on it. After a hug, a handshake and wave, I pedaled off up Route 55.

My first day of solo riding started out cool and overcast with no wind. I missed having Jim's company, but riding solo wasn't so bad. I sang, did math problems in my head, planned my day and watched for birds. The bike felt good. I felt good. After a few hours, the wind increased, but it was a tail wind propelling me at 18 to 20 mph.

I passed a fellow mowing his grass. The fresh-cut grass smelled so sweet. On one break I stopped by a freshly plowed field and smelled fresh-turned dirt. The smell reminded me of when I was a kid digging in the dirt. Back then, I thought dirt smelled so good I ate it. When I rode past the lilac bushes, the sweet scent from the blossoms was overpowering.

During a snack stop at a gas station, I saw Mallo Cups, a milk-chocolate cup filled with creamy marshmallow, on the candy rack. That was my favorite candy when I was a kid, but I hadn't seen them in the store for 45 years. I bought one, bit into it and savored the sweet, creamy taste. It was as good as I remembered. That's unusual because most of my childhood favorites are now disappointing.

A train passed me late in the day going about 30 mph. I was riding 20 mph counting the freight cars as they passed. The train slowed down to switch onto a siding; I caught up and passed it. Train chasing kept me busy for 30 or 40 minutes and provided a pleasant diversion.

The Minnesota terrain from Minneapolis to Glenwood is as flat as Central Illinois with only the occasional small hill. It is great for biking. With a slight tail wind, I could pedal in high gear up the hills at 15 mph and make 20 mph on the flat stretches.

It was exciting to watch the bike's odometer roll through 999.7 miles, 999.8, 999.9 and clicked over to 1000.0 before I reached the motel. After pedaling along the road alone for ten hours a day, it didn't take much to get me excited.

Saturday started out cool, cloudy and foggy with a light southeast wind. I felt good, but was concerned about the possibility of more bike problems and flat tires. The road was concrete covered with asphalt and had a wide shoulder that I rode on. There were concrete joints every 20 feet. The thin asphalt layer didn't completely cover the joint so my bike gave me a jolt every time I crossed them. In a 100-mile ride there are 25,000 joints. That means my bottom was jolted 25,000 times that day. Any wonder it was a little tender?

Minnesota advertises they are the land of 10,000 lakes. I passed small lakes, big lakes, wide lakes, skinny lakes, grassy lakes, clear lakes, blue lakes and green lakes. At one point I tried to count them, but couldn't figure out what came after "one trillion."

At Elbow Lake, I stopped for a second breakfast at a small café. While I was eating my bacon and eggs, an older gentleman in overalls came in and sat down at the next table. He saw my biking outfit and asked where I was going.

"Alaska," I said.

"Are you going to ride that skinny-tired bike I saw parked out front all the way to Alaska?"

"No, I'll switch to a mountain bike when I hit the bad, gravel road along the Alaskan Highway."

"I had a bike when I was a kid," he said with that long-ago, pleasant-memory look in his eyes. "We rode down muddy dirt roads with big ruts in them. When we got to the gravel road, we thought that was the *good* road. I guess it all depends on your point of view."

After Elbow Lake, the hills grew bigger, but the wind was still to my back so there was no problem riding up them. I entered Otter Tail County and rode into Fergus Falls about noon. Along the river I spied a giant otter, over 20 feet tall in Otter Tail Park. After taking a quick photo, I continued up Union Street. The wide street was lined with 50-year-old walnut trees, two in front of each house. It was like a scene out of a movie. The well-preserved houses were beautiful, each with an immaculately manicured lawn. These weren't mansions, just nice big homes with interesting old architecture and nicely landscaped yards. I think it is the prettiest street I've ever seen.

Old Route 52 was narrow and bumpy on the way out of Fergus Falls. The wind shifted and blew directly in my face. My speed slowed to 11 or 12 mph; my spirits sagged. The sun came out and it became very hot. I spent four hours dodging cars and potholes, bucking the wind and fighting dragons.

Somehow I miscalculated the distance from Fergus Falls to Fargo. It turned out to be 20 miles further than my estimate. Coupled with the bad road, it felt like an extra 100 miles.

When I finally reached Moorhead, Minnesota, I had trouble finding my way through town into Fargo, North Dakota. I called the friend I was to stay with in Fargo, Elvin (Is) Isgrig. He provided me directions through an industrial park and residential area to a bicycle bridge across the Red River in Gooseberry Park. I rode through the park and met Is by the bridge. He took my photo crossing into North Dakota.

I was surprised at how narrow the Red River is. From the movies I've seen and stories I've read about the Red River, I was expecting to find a huge gorge and a big, roaring river. At Gooseberry Park, the river is only about 40-feet wide, not as big as our Great Miami River in Dayton. The other surprising thing is that the Red River flows north into Canada, running through Lake Winnipeg and then into Hudson Bay! I thought all the rivers in the Mid-West flowed south.

Twenty minutes past the Red River, I biked into Isgrig's garage and completed the longest ride of my life, 125 miles in 10 hours.

After a hot, soaking bath I spent the evening reminiscing about the Air Force communication projects we worked on 30 years ago, talking about grandchildren and discussing the solutions to all of the world's problems with Is, his wife, Carol, and another avid biker, Shaun Lynch. During a lull in the conversation, I asked where Fargo got its name.

"The town was named for William Fargo, a director for the Northern Pacific Railroad and founder of Wells Fargo Express Company," Is explained. "The town sprung up in 1871 when the Northern Pacific Railroad built a bridge across the Red River from Moorhead and started laying track on the North Dakota side. The land was still Sioux Indian Territory at the

Allen crossing the Red River into Fargo, North Dakota

time. North Dakota didn't become a state until 1889. There were originally two tent communities, 'Fargo on the Prairie' and 'Fargo in the Timber.' 'Fargo on the Prairie' was headquarters for the railroad. The engineers, surveyors and their families lived there in a rather nice frontier settlement near the present corner of Broadway and Front streets. 'Fargo in the Timber' was a rough settlement along the river where the workers and camp followers lived. It was best known for gunfights and whiskey."

"What's the population of Fargo?"

"It's about 74,000 now," Is replied. "There are only four cities in North Dakota with a population over 25,000; Fargo, Grand Forks, Bismarck and Minot. The whole state only has 600,000 people."

On Sunday, Carol, Is and I attended the Methodist Church service where the congregation said a special prayer for a safe bike trip. At the Heritage Hjemkomst Interpretative Center we toured a beautiful, full-size replica of a wooden Viking sailing ship that was built in a nearby shipyard. A North Dakota crew of 13 and a Norwegian skipper sailed the ship through the Great Lakes and across the Atlantic to Norway to celebrate the Viking's sailing to the New World.

The TV news reporter, Eric Hanson, from KXJB came over Sunday afternoon for an interview. He took pictures of me working on my bike in Isgrig's backyard and asked the usual questions: What, when, where, how and why.

Carol washed and dried my clothes Sunday evening so I'd have a clean outfit to ride in. I wore the same biking shirt and shorts every day of the trip, rinsing them out every night in my motel. It was nice to have them run through a real washing machine occasionally.

"The North Dakota country roads you're planning to ride are short on eating places," Carol warned me at breakfast Monday morning. "We drive that same route every few weeks to visit Is' folks and the road is pretty desolate. Let me fix you a lunch. Is a turkey sandwich okay?"

"Turkey is my favorite," I said.

After breakfast, we watched the bike interview on TV. Eric had run it on the 10 o'clock news Sunday night and Is taped it. He included the video Is had taken of me riding into Fargo and across the Red River on Saturday and even used some photos from my web site[1] showing granddaughter Kelsey and I rollerblading across Holland.

I felt relaxed and confident as I rode north out of Fargo up old Route 81 on a calm, cool, sunny morning. The good Lord must have thought that the previous week's tail wind was making me a little too cocky and He decided to give me some humility in the form of a light head wind right on my nose. My speed dropped from 13 to 12 to 11 to 10 to 9 mph as the head

---

[1] www.creative-enterprises.org

wind picked up and my confidence dropped. When I turned west at Gardner, I expected to have the wind from the side. No, the wind shifted to the northwest and was still almost a direct head wind. I struggled along at 9 or 10 mph. When I stopped at a Sinclair station outside of Gardner for a snack, a flatbed truck pulled in with a Plymouth Prowler on the back. The driver said he was taking the racy $60,000 car to the Swift River Casino at Devil's Lake where it would be raffled off.

Good thing Carol packed me a lunch because my route was definitely desolate. I really appreciated the sandwich, cookies and apple; that was all I had to eat that afternoon. I watched one dark cloud form in the sky directly in front of me, building up bigger and higher as it headed straight my way. I stopped and put my poncho on just as the sky opened up. It rained cats and dogs for a solid hour. The wind picked up and I struggled to make 6 to 8 mph. After the rain stopped, the sun came out again. I was out of sunscreen and ended up lobster red with a good sun/wind burn at the end of the day.

The land around Gardner was basically flat with an occasional small hill. My usual routine was to ride along singing, daydreaming and fantasizing to take my mind off the pedaling. It wasn't working this day. I was concentrating on the wind, the hills and turning the pedals, which changed a pleasant bike ride into hard work. Near Cooperstown, I encountered a few more hills and one huge gully where Sheyenne River cut through. It was steep enough on the uphill portion to have a truck lane. I huffed and puffed my way up that hill at 5 mph. Finally at 7 p.m., after 115 miles and 12.5 hours of hard pedaling, I struggled into Glenfield, two hours behind my expected schedule. This was my toughest day of the trip so far. Mother told me hard work built character, and this day I spent 12.5 hours character building.

I stopped to visit Elvy and Dorothy Isgrig, the parents of my friends in Fargo. They live in a small yellow house, which Elvy bought for $50 back in 1941. He worked as a lumberjack in Wisconsin, farm hand in North Dakota, ran a grocery and worked on the railroad before he retired and took up upholstering. Dorothy ran the grocery store and raised the family. She is an expert seamstress and does the mending for the entire village of Glenfield. At age 70 she learned to upholster and started writing the village news for two nearby papers. Now in their nineties, the Isgrigs continue to upholster furniture and weave rag rugs on the loom in their garage, "to keep themselves busy."

The smell of the meal cooking piqued my appetite and by the time the Isgrigs and I sat down to the scrumptious supper of roast pork, mashed potatoes, creamed green beans and cranberry sauce, I was famished. Mrs. Isgrig baked rhubarb pie for dessert and served it with ice cream. I thought I'd died and gone to heaven. After supper we sat in the parlor, drank a cup of tea and talked.

"Dug our well by hand," Elvy said. "It's 40-feet deep. Used a post-hole digger with an extension. The old well used to go dry if we had company--too many people flushing the toilet and taking baths."

"We're covering a davenport for our preacher now," Dorothy said. "It's an unusual one with odd-shaped arms. Boy, will I be glad when it's done and on the truck back to James River."

They are a fascinating couple and I asked how they met.

"Dorothy was the boss's daughter when I worked on Mr. Overbeck's farm," Elvy said. "I ran the steam-engine threshing machine there. Dorothy and I went to Moorhead to get married. The preacher mixed up the names on the marriage certificate with another couple who were getting married at the same time. We had to go back and have him make a new certificate."

"Have you always lived in Glenfield?" I asked.

"I was born in Iowa, but moved to Glenfield when I was a little girl," Dorothy said. "After we married, I ran a grocery store here. I remember one day I was driving our Model A Ford around town to pick up some supplies and it started making an awful noise. I drove into the Chevy dealer. Everyone in the garage came over to see the car; it was making such a racket. It had thrown three rods (a Model A only had four cylinders and, therefore, only four rods). We had to trade it in and get a new car."

The bike adventure was turning into a nostalgic trip. I started the ride with Jim Coppola, an Air Force Flight Test Engineer who worked with me ten years ago. The first night we had supper with my high school classmate of 45 years ago. In Illinois, I stopped and visited with a childhood sweetheart from 46 years ago. When we reached Minneapolis, I stayed with a friend who was the Flight Test Director on my Air Force communications project in 1970. In Fargo I spent the weekend with the retired Air Force colonel who directed our project back in 1967. Add to that the old-fashioned A&W root beer stand in Plattsville and the Burma Shave sign I saw outside of Galena. Reliving those great memories added immense pleasure to the ride.

CHAPTER 5

INTERROGATION AT THE CANADIAN BORDER

Dorothy fixed a delightful breakfast of waffles, eggs and pork sausage. There were hugs and hearty handshakes all around as I prepared to leave. I felt as though I'd known the Isgrigs all my life. The morning dawned cool and sunny with no wind as I rode west from Glenfield at 15 mph. Many of the green fields of wheat had a foot of water standing in them and flocks of mallard ducks, with their iridescent-green heads, paddling around.

A traditional prairie Lutheran Church stood on the hill, the classic one-room white building silhouetted against the dark blue sky. It was closed, but in good repair. The sign announced "James River Landmark and Lutheran Cemetery." A lady in the next town told me they still used the church occasionally for a baptism or wedding.

In Carrington, I stopped at an Amoco gas station for a snack of Ritz Air Crisps and a Pepsi. Sitting with the clerk, Mary and her friend, Dorothy, at the only table in the station, we discussed my quest. Mary was impressed. She gave me a container of nacho cheese to dip my crisps in.

"You need more than dry chips to make the next hundred miles," Mary said.

The bright sun in my face reminded me to get a bottle of sunscreen at the drug store. Ten dollars for a small bottle, expensive--but essential. Out of Carrington, the road turned

36

north and I flew along at 20 mph with a tail wind. I pedaled into Fessenden and AJ's Motel, my destination, about 1:00 p.m., covering the 66 miles in 6 hours. It was a great day of riding and the fourth day in a row without a flat tire. Things were definitely looking up.

AJ's is a small, old-fashioned motel. My room was just wide enough for the bed and a door. It was small, but clean, comfortable, quiet and economically priced at $21 a night.

For lunch, I walked to the Filling Station, a pleasant restaurant, and ordered a delicious bowl of Kreiffla soup: German dumplings, chicken broth stock, carrots, onions and basil. After lunch I took a nap and then worked on my journal.

I'd ridden over 1,000 miles to Fessenden and the bike was taking a beating. In the evening I fussed with the bicycle: oiled the chain, tightened all the screws, wiped the dirt off and looked for undetected problems. Other than the broken spoke, I had experienced no mechanical problems with the bike--just a lot of flat tires.

On Wednesday, I headed for Minot with a slight tail wind, riding 16-20 mph. This was my first morning without breakfast. AJ's didn't have a restaurant and nothing was open in Fessenden at 6:00 a.m. My route crossed the Continental Divide (1616 feet above sea level) near the village of Harvey. The town boosters had erected a big statue of King Kong, 40 feet high, and a sign announcing: "Welcome to Harvey. Not even a gorilla can stop a Harvey Hornet!"

JW's Restaurant, the first opportunity for breakfast, materialized at the edge of Harvey. Six men wearing farmer's overalls sat in one dining room drinking coffee and gossiping. Four women wearing colorful sweat suits sat in the adjacent room drinking their morning coffee and talking. The men were talking about farming and the effect of the floodwaters. The women were chatting about other women. I chose the room occupied by the men and ordered hot oatmeal, a bagel, fruit and tea. While eating breakfast I overheard conversations about the current price of wheat, what the export market prospects were and how the war in Bosnia was affecting crop prices.

"Where are you headed?" one of the farmers asked during a lull in their conversation.

"Alaska."

That immediately changed the farmers' conversation to biking. I explained my Arctic Circle trip and the Salvation Army pledge connection. The farmers passed a hat around their table for the Salvation Army and brought the donation over to me.

Beautiful black birds sang a melodious, multi-tone song as I biked past the small farm ponds. I had never seen the birds before, not even in bird books. They are black birds, a little bigger than a redwing black bird. These birds have yellow feathers on their chest, shoulders and head and a white semicircle on the leading edge of their wings (where a redwing has red and yellow). They populate the swamps and lakes next to the road along with the redwing black bird. Maybe it is a new species of bird, a mutation from the redwing black bird caused by atomic radiation.

While I was concentrating on the black bird's song, a long iridescent-green snake slithered across the road in front of me. I had to swerve sharply to avoid hitting it. Can you imagine this snake wrapped around the bike wheels like the crepe paper streamers children weave through the spokes for a parade?

The floodwaters were still high in North Dakota, a result of six inches of rain the previous week. Around Balfour, a steady stream of water 12-inches deep was running across the road for a distance of 100 yards. There seemed no way around it so I rode down the centerline of the highway through the ice-cold water. My shoes and pant legs were soaked and the water didn't do my chain and bearings much good.

The land from Glenfield to Harvey was so flat I could see 20 or 30 miles to the distant horizon in all directions. Approaching Velva, the terrain became quite hilly. That limited visibility to a mile or less in all directions because of the small, abrupt hills. The railroad still curves along the valley floor, but the highway went straight up and down the 300-foot high hills. The sun came out, warming things considerably and I started sweating while pedaling up those hills.

There were 40 old threshing machines parked in a field near Velva. They looked like a herd of metal dinosaurs, standing, waiting patiently to be hooked up to a steam engine or tractor drive-wheel. I always thought the thresher moved through the field to process the wheat, but Elvy Isgrig told me the steam engine and the thresher stood still and hired hands brought the wheat to the machine to be processed. Technical progress and giant combines made the threshing machines obsolete.

Minot appeared on the horizon about mid-afternoon. I didn't know where the motel was located so I stopped at the edge of town at an auto-parts store and asked.   This was totally against the normal, manly instinct of "never ask directions--just keep driving around in circles and you'll find what you're looking for." The lady in the store directed me to the other side of town. It was convenient for the motel to be on the other side of town as that provided a fast start out of town the next day, but today I was tired and was hoping the motel was at the south edge of town. Anyhow, this was a relatively short day of biking: 93 miles in 8 hours.

When I registered at the motel, the clerk asked my destination so I handed her a copy of my Arctic Circle news release.   Later in the evening the night clerk, a middle-aged gentleman, knocked on my door.

"I read your write-up," he said.   "That's a fantastic adventure. Here's $20 for the Salvation Army. You'll be in my prayers."

"Thank you very much," I said. Then I went to bed.

My typical day on tour starts when the alarm goes off at 4:00 a.m. I dress and work on my daily notes or weekly summary. Then I log on the Internet and check my e-mail. At

6:00, the restaurant opens so I eat breakfast, then brush my teeth, pack up and am on the road by 6:30 or 7:00 a.m. My first break is between 9:00 and 10:00 a.m.--whenever I find a gas station or restaurant to buy a snack. I pedal until noon and stop for lunch. In the afternoon, I stop for a snack and rest about every two hours. I usually arrive at my motel between 4:00 and 7:00 p.m. My first order of business is a hot, soaking bath to relax the tired muscles. Then I work on notes until supper time. After supper I oil the bike, tighten all the nuts and bolts and look for unusual wear on the chain, tires and moving parts. Sometimes I watch CNN Headline News for 30 minutes to catch up on world happenings. Finally, I work on my notes until bedtime--9:30 p.m.

The road followed the valley as I pedaled out of Minot Thursday morning with 200-foot-high hills on each side. My speed was 7-9 mph riding directly into a 20-knot head wind, like going uphill all the time and never getting out of my middle gear. The nearby hills were speckled with white stones. Local high school kids have arranged the stones on hills along a 30-mile stretch of the highway to indicate the year they graduated, 1953 to the present. That's a better idea than painting the dates on the side of concrete bridges.

I stopped at the Quik Stop in Donnybrook for lunch and met Gerry Helmers, who owns the gas station and also farms.

"This afternoon I plan to pick rocks out of one of my fields while my brother watches the store," he said.

"Have you always living in Donnybrook?" I asked.

"Yeah, I was born here," Gerry said. "Donnybrook has low crime and friendly, helpful people. If I did something wrong when I was a kid, my mother knew about it before I got home. My brother and I used to bike a lot when we were kids. One day when I was about 10 years old, we decided to bike to Kenmare (15 miles away), where Dad was working, and ride home with him in his truck. Mom grounded us when she found out we rode up the highway without permission. She put our bikes on the shed roof."

"How big is Kenmare?"

"It's pretty big. Probably 10 or 12 hundred people." I thought Gerry was going to say 10 or 12 thousand, but there are only 7 cities with a population over 10,000 in all of North Dakota.

"Not many fat people in the small towns of North Dakota," I said.

"Naw. We have too many chores to get fat, and we don't have any fast food restaurants near by."

The wind was so strong as I rode out of Donnybrook that even the ducks were grounded. They usually fly away as I pedal up to a pond, but this day, they just swam to the other side of the pond and waddled over to the next one.

It was about 2:00 p.m. when I pedaled into Kenmare. A dozen cars, each carrying five or six high school kids, were driving up and down the street honking their horns and yelling out the windows. It was May 20th and they were celebrating the last day of the school year in North Dakota. I thought my granddaughter in Missouri finished school early--May 27th.

The head wind was still strong outside of Kenmare. I was fighting the demons all afternoon, and it was hard to think pleasant thoughts or enjoy biking with a 20-knot wind blowing directly in my face. To combat the demons, I've developed several techniques to occupy my mind. In his book, Psycho-Cybernetics (Maltz, 1960), Maxwell Maltz equates the functioning of the human body to a servomechanism. He contends that your mind doesn't need to continuously direct your legs to "push down now on the right pedal and pull up now on the left pedal." According to Maltz, you set a goal in your subconscious mind of moving the bike forward and then your subconscious directs the various muscles in the right sequence to turn the pedals at the proper time. I found what Maltz said to be absolutely true. I could ride for an hour and never once give a conscious thought to pedaling. As a matter of fact, if I thought about it, I couldn't tell exactly where my feet were at any given time. It was as though my legs were detached from my body and going around and around by themselves.

To occupy my mind, I daydream about some pleasant situation. One of my favorite daydreams was to pick out a farmhouse I was passing and imagine stopping there and knocking on the front door. A gray-haired, grandmotherly lady with a yellow pinafore apron would answer the door and invite me in. We would go into her kitchen and sit down at a large, round oak table. As we talked about family and relatives, she would pour me a cup of orange-spice Constant Comment tea and offer me a plate of warm, fresh-baked bread. I'd smear some creamery butter on the bread and then cover it with raspberry jam. My mouth would actually water as I imagined biting into the bread and washing it down with a sip of hot tea.

She would tell me about all the interesting things her children and grandchildren were doing and I would tell her stories about my children and grandchildren. Then we would reminisce about the good old days when everything happened at a slower pace. When I finished my tea I would thank her, walk to the front door, get on my bike and ride away. She would always invite me to stop back anytime.

Another diversion I used to pass the time was to repeat my "Golden Words." Years ago I saw the movie "Cinderella" with Leslie Caron, Michael Rennie and Mildred Natwick. Mildred Natwick walked around dusting the dining room table with her long-haired cat saying "apple dumpling" and other phrases because she thought those words had a pretty sound. Over the years I collected the following words that I think sound pretty and invoke pleasant thoughts:

Kailua	*Tranquil*	*Butterscotch*
Dawn	*Rainbow*	*Maple sugar*
Misty	*Smile*	*Billabong*
Golden	*Heather*	*Wabash*

As I rode along repeating those words, a pleasant image would come to mind. It would take me several minutes to run completely through my list of golden words and I would repeat them several times.

Late in the day I would start daydreaming about the hot bath that awaited me at the end of each day's ride. I'd visualize pedaling up to the hotel, registering, walking to my room, running a tub of hot water, undressing and sliding into a hot bath. I could feel the hot water relaxing my tired leg muscles as I soaked in the tub. I sometimes think my imaginary bath was as relaxing as the real one.

It was 7:30 p.m. when I finally arrived in Portal and located the Americana Motel. The only restaurant in this town of 192 people closed at 7:00 p.m. so to add insult to injury I didn't get supper this night. A Pepsi and a bag of potato chips from the vending machine were my reward for biking 93 miles in 12.5 hours. This was my slowest and toughest day yet. Good thing I was committed to meeting my niece in Saskatchewan or I would have been tempted to call the whole trip off at this point and take the bus back home.

I felt better Friday morning after a good night's sleep, but there was no place to get breakfast in Portal. The Canadian Immigration officer asked me to park my bike and step into the building at the U.S./Canada border that runs through Portal. It was 6:00 a.m. and there were no other tourists there, just the Canadian officials and me. They asked a lot of questions:

"What is your citizenship?" – "U.S."

"Have you been in Canada before?" – "Yes."

"What are you bringing into Canada?" – "My bike, clothes, tools, maps and computer."

"How much money do you have with you?" – "$300."

"How long do you expect to stay?" – "Four weeks."

"Is this a business or pleasure trip?" – "Pleasure."

"What is your destination?" – "Alaska."

43

"Do you have credit cards?" – "Yes." (They demanded I show them the credit cards.)

"Have you ever been in jail?" – "No."

"Have you been fingerprinted?" – "Yes, for my government security clearance."

"Have you ever been refused entry into Canada?" "No."

"Are you carrying any fruit, guns, drugs or cigarettes?" – "No."

I've driven across the Canadian border dozens of times and the officials only asked where I was going and how long I would be staying. Biking across must be unusual and they appeared to be afraid I wouldn't make it out of Canada. After a 15-minute question and answer session, the officials finally decided it was safe to let me enter their country.

"Have a nice day," the Canadian immigration officer said as I left.

The interrogation made me feel I was going into a hostile foreign country rather than our closest neighbor with the longest unprotected border in the world.

Once safely across the border, I rode through an extensive coal strip-mining area. In every direction I looked there were giant shovels scooping the dirt off the coal---at least a dozen of them. One of the gargantuan shovels was digging right alongside the road. The cab on the shovel, which houses the operator and motors, is the size of my two-story house and the dragline bucket is as big as my two-car garage. The shovel took huge bites out of the ground in front of it, swung around and deposited the mound of dirt in a pile behind it. There was a visitor's information center a few miles beyond the shovel that displayed a dragline bucket. I stopped and took a picture of the bike and me in one of the buckets that can hold 43 cubic yards of material. BIG!

The weather turned cold (45 degrees) and windy. It started raining about an hour into Canada so I put my poncho on over my Gore-Tex jacket to keep warm. I was making good

The strip-mining shovel bucket is as big as a garage.

time with the wind to my back, 16-20 mph. About 8:00 a.m. I pedaled into the first Canadian town with a restaurant, Estevan, Saskatchewan, and stopped for a big breakfast of French toast, bacon, orange juice and hot tea. After breakfast I biked to a Seven-Eleven store and used their Automatic Teller Machine (ATM) to get $400 in Canadian currency. The exchange rate was good---about 65 cents American to $1 Canadian.

The cold rain stung my face as I biked out of Estevan. After three hours of fighting the rain and the wind I reached Midale, chilled to the bone. My first priority was someplace dry and warm that served hot food. The Midale Café looked like it would satisfy all my requirements.

"Give me a big bowl of chicken-rice soup," I told the waitress.

45

The steaming-hot bowl of homemade soup hit the spot! These small restaurants with their homemade specialties are a delight. Much better selections than the fast-food chains. It had a hand-lettered sign on the wall advertising a special seafood diet:

"If I see food, I eat it!"

As I ate the hot soup, I could feel the blood flowing up through my arms; into my hands; down my legs and into my feet bringing soothing warmth to my chilled fingers and toes. Once my belly was full and my hands and feet were warm I almost fell asleep at the table. A cup of tea and a piece of hot apple pie topped off a delightful meal and woke me up. Totally refreshed, I pedaled out of Midale with the wind to my back and raced into Weyburn just after noon--my shortest day of biking yet. The good Lord spared me two hard days in a row.

After unpacking the bike, I plugged my computer into the motel telephone line to check my e-mail. It took a half hour to find the Canadian America On Line (AOL) toll-free telephone number, but I eventually got on-line and read my e-mail. Verio, the web site provider, had finally updated my web-site newsletter with the bike-trip weekly summary. After soaking my tired muscles in a hot bath, I oiled my bicycle, wiped the mud and water off and checked all the bolts/screws for tightness. The next day would be another early morning start and none of the restaurants opened early so I walked down to a grocery store and bought cereal, milk and yogurt for breakfast. I don't like starting out in the morning without something to eat. Breakfast is my favorite meal and I needed to fuel up before getting on the road.

The morning was cold (45 degrees) and raining as I started at 6:00 a.m. for Regina wearing my Gore-Tex pants and jacket with my rain poncho on top. All of me was toasty warm except my fingers and toes. The land was absolutely flat for the 75 miles between Weyburn and Regina--not a single hill. My top speed for the entire day was 17 mph down a slight incline.

Halfway to Regina, I stopped at a historic monument dedicated to the 250-mile trail from Wood Mountain to Fort Qu'appelle which passed this way. The sign said that in the 1850s Indians, hunters, traders, missionaries, mounted police and pioneers transported pelts, pemmican and provisions over this trail. The Indian leader, Sitting Bull, led the remainder of his Sioux Indian band this way, vainly seeking sanctuary in the Qu'appelle Valley. Wagon trains with furs and meat made the trip in about three weeks. I was riding the same trail in about three days, but the road is much better today.

I rode past the Regina city limits about noon and stopped to take a picture of the beautiful "Welcome to Regina, Home of the RCMP," sign. The Royal Canadian Mounted Police first came to this area in 1875 to quell a Cree rebellion. At that time there were only 150 Mounties in all of Canada. Regina subsequently became the home or depot for the RCMP.

As I pulled off the road onto the dirt shoulder to take a photo, I discovered the shoulder consisted of sticky six-inch deep mud. The tires of my bike sank down in the mud instantly, and I lost my balance. Before I could unclip my bike-shoes from the pedals, the bike and I keeled over into the gooey mud. It was another Charlie Chaplin slapstick routine. Me wallowing around in the sticky, muddy mess trying to get my feet loose from the pedals. When I was finally free, I slowly extracted myself from the mud and then retrieved my bike. I spent 30 minutes scraping mud off the bike and me as people drove by pointing, laughing and shouting words of encouragement. Then I pedaled to McDonald's and used their restroom to wash up. I never did get a photo of the welcome sign! After cleaning up the best I could, I pedaled through Regina toward the In-Towner Motel on the north edge of Regina.

The area around Regina was settled in 1872 when the Dominion Lands Act encouraged homesteaders to come to this rich-soil farming area. The Cree Indians had hunted this area for years as the huge piles of buffalo bones attested. They piled the bones up in belief that the buffalo would not leave the area where other buffalo died. The first settlement was known as Wascana, or "pile of bones" in Cree. In 1882, the town's name was changed to Regina, Latin for Queen, by Princess Louise, wife of the Governor General of Canada and daughter of Queen Victoria. The capital of the Northwest Territory was moved from Battleford in 1883 to Regina. In 1905, Saskatchewan became a Province with Regina its capital.

The "Queen City" is a beautiful town of 160,000 people with elegant homes and interesting museums, art galleries, science centers, parks and stately government buildings. As I pedaled up Albert Street I passed the 2,300-acre Wascana Park, the largest urban park in North America. The Saskatchewan Legislative Building is at the heart of Wascana Center, overlooking picturesque Wascana Lake.

Arriving at the motel, I checked in and retrieved the road bicycle Gloria had shipped up for Karen to ride. After a hot bath to wash the mud off, I assembled Karen's bike and then washed my muddy clothes in the guest laundry. Next, I cleaned the remaining mud from my bike and oiled the chain.

My niece, Karen Johnson, flew into Regina from Boulder, Colorado Saturday evening. She planned to ride with me for six days from Regina, Saskatchewan, to Edmonton, Alberta. After supper Karen tried out the bike, riding around the parking lot. Her feet didn't reach the ground when she was on the seat.

"I think the seat needs to be a little bit lower," Karen said. "Other than that, the bike feels great."

CHAPTER 6
WHAT IS A SASKATOON TORT?

"Regina is a beautiful city with wonderful parks and excellent weather," the Polish lady who ran the motel restaurant said, as Karen and I ate an early breakfast. My ride into the city gave me the same impression.

Karen and I biked through the sleepy city on a crisp Sunday morning and out onto the eight-foot wide shoulder of a four-lane divided highway. Karen, who practiced on a mountain bike in Colorado, got the knack of riding the skinny-tired road bike right away. She shifted the gears up and down effectively as we rode the small hills outside of Regina.

At Lumsden we shot down into Qu'Appelle Valley, a 300-foot deep green gorge, at 35 mph and back up at 6 mph. The weather was cool and cloudy with a light rain, but by the time we biked out of the valley, both Karen and I were sweating. We rode at 15-18 mph on the flat land with no wind. A head wind blew in around 8:30 a.m. and slowed us down to 11 mph. The heat-driven wind increased hourly. Karen took off her long-sleeved shirt at 9:00 a.m. and her jacket at 10:00 a.m., leaving her in a short-sleeved biking shirt and shorts. If the temperature continued to warm up, I expected she would be down to a bikini by noon.

The head wind continued to increase, slowing us to 7 mph average and sometimes 5 mph top speed in gusts. It was Sunday and I think the good Lord was displeased that we were biking on the Sabbath. When the wind let up for a minute allowing us to speed up to 10 mph, I felt like we were traveling

Karen's and Allen's bikes loaded with their clothes and gear.

at the speed of sound! We continued up and down small hills all morning and by mid-day, Karen's legs were getting tired and sore.

"I don't think I can continue for another 40 miles against this wind," she said when we stopped at an Esso station in Chamberlain around 2:00 p.m. for a snack. "I didn't know it could be so much work riding into the wind."

"We have a couple of options," I said. "One would be to look for a room here in Chamberlain and another is to see if there is anyone headed for Davidson where our original motel is located. What do you think about continuing to Davidson in a car?"

"That would be okay," Karen said.

John, one of the young service station attendants, was about to finish work and he agreed to drive Karen to Davidson if

I paid for his gas. Settled. He loaded Karen's bike in his trunk and they started for Davidson.

I mounted my bike and pedaled toward our destination at 7 mph with my head down to reduce the aerodynamic drag. Riding that way limited my visibility to a five-foot stretch of asphalt pavement. This was not my idea of great bike touring, but it did decrease my drag. Every 30 minutes I'd stop for a drink of water and to eat one of the snacks I was carrying in my saddlebags. I consumed all my snack food and emptied three bottles of water during the 40-mile ride. At Craik, the welcome sign claimed, "The Friendliest Place by a Dam Site." I stopped at the Craik Restaurant for a more substantial snack. The daily special beef hot-shot sandwich looked delicious as the waitress served it to the couple at the next table.

"I'll have the same," I told the waitress.

The people in the restaurant lived up to the sign's "friendly" claim. They asked my destination, gave me advice on where to eat in Davidson and commiserated about the windy weather.

"Worst wind we've had this spring," a gentleman in a green John Deere baseball cap said.

The wind started to die down about 6:30 p.m. and I could sprint at Mach 2 (15 mph). I finally pedaled into Davidson at 7:30 p.m. and met Karen who was eating a cheese pizza in the snack bar at our motel. It was a relief to see that Karen had no ill effects from her strenuous seven-hour bike ride.

"We got to the motel about 3 o'clock," she told me. "I soaked in the tub and took a nap till 7 o'clock. Now I feel great."

I ordered a bowl of hamburger-vegetable soup. The crisp vegetables, chunky hamburger and hot, thick broth made a delicious meal. After supper I made a phone call home to Gloria.

"It's after 10 o'clock," Gloria said. "I was starting to worry when you didn't call by 7 o'clock."

"There's a two-hour time difference between Dayton and here," I explained. "I just got in a half hour ago. Everything's going okay. We had a terrible head wind today and the ride took longer than expected."

After the phone call I went to my room and took a hot, soaking bath. My thigh and calf muscles let me know they were not pleased with the extended workout. It was about 10 o'clock when I finally collapsed into the bed, ending the most exhausting day of my trip so far, 90 miles in 12.5 hours.

Karen agreed to get up early Monday morning to try and beat the wind that seemed to increase mid-day. We were up at 4:00 a.m., ate cereal we had bought the night before at the snack bar and were on the road just after sunrise at 5:00 a.m. Surprisingly, Karen was feeling good, with no sore muscles as we biked along the divided highway. The sun was up, but the weather was partly cloudy and cool.

"It's fun riding with no wind and no traffic," Karen said as we rode along side-by-side and chatted.

"Yes, life can be beautiful when the wind dies down," I agreed.

One of the advantages of a long bike ride with my niece was that I had plenty of time to talk to her and learn more about her hopes and dreams.

"I don't plan to live in Boulder all my life," she said. "I'd like to move to the East Coast or West Coast sometime to see what those areas are like."

"Have you met anyone special in Boulder?" I asked.

"Yes, Jeff. I met him at a writers support group. He's an only child and a vegetarian like myself. When I took him to the Texas A&M alumni dinner in Denver, we were the only two people who had requested vegetarian meals out of the crowd of about 300. Texas Aggies are steak eaters."

"Where does he work?"

Saskatoon has a beautiful bikeway along the river.

"He's a chemical engineer for a medical company that makes heart pumps and special medical equipment."

"What does Jeff like to do?"

"He likes the outdoors: mountain biking, hiking, skiing, snowshoeing and swimming."[1]

With the help of a slight tail wind, we were halfway to Saskatoon, our destination, by 7:30 a.m. We stopped in Henley for a waffle breakfast with real maple syrup. After breakfast, the road dropped down into the Blackstrap Valley alongside a big reservoir ten miles long and half a mile wide. Most of our route was along treeless plains of wheat fields, but the

---

[1]On New Year's day 2000 while Karen and Jeff were snowshoeing through the Rocky Mountains of Colorado, he got down on one knee and proposed marriage to Karen. The wedding is planned for June 2000.

Blackstrap Valley contained a wide, green forested game preserve that ran for 15 or 20 miles along the Brightwater River.

We flew along the road at 20 to 30 mph all morning, thanks to a strong tail wind. By 11:00 a.m. Karen led me into the outskirts of Saskatoon, our destination. Our route took us onto the heavily congested Circle Drive, commonly referred to as *the Indy 500 speedway.* We immediately exited the speedway, turning off onto city streets. A local resident directed us along the residential streets to the bikeway beside the South Saskatchewan River. The bikeway is a beautiful trail with residential and university buildings on the southeast side where we were riding and downtown buildings on the northwest side. The bikeway looked a lot like the one in Dayton along the Great Miami River. Karen and I stopped at the International Peace Prayer Post to take pictures and say a prayer. The inscription on the monument explained its purpose:

"The Peace Prayer Pole is a part of a worldwide tradition of similar poles meant to encourage people to visualize, pray and work for world peace. The tradition, supported by the United Nations, originated in Japan and has spread to 160 countries. The message is written in English, French, Japanese and Cree."

After crossing the University Bridge, we stopped near the dam to watch the white pelicans dive for fish. I thought pelicans lived in Florida! That stop gave us an opportunity to talk to some of the joggers, bikers and rollerbladers using the busy bikeway. We then pedaled through another residential area to the Country Inn on the north side of Saskatoon. We had completed the 77-mile ride in 6 hours and were as happy as a couple of big sunflowers.

"Now this is what long-distance bike touring is supposed to be like," Karen said.

Saskatoon is Saskatchewan's second largest city, named after the Saskatoon berries common in that area. Pioneers from Ontario founded Saskatoon in 1883 as a temperance colony. The city was developed with planned open space for parks along both sides of the river and throughout the city. Modern office buildings, attractive homes and the University of Saskatchewan campus make Saskatoon one of the most beautiful cities in Canada.

For supper we ate in an elegant, mirrored dining room in the Travel Lodge Motel. Karen ordered meatless fettuccini Alfredo. I ate roast turkey with dressing and mashed potatoes. The restaurant's special dessert was a Saskatoon torte.

"What is a Saskatoon torte?" I asked.

"It's like a Saskatoon pie but it's a cake," the waitress replied.

"What's a Saskatoon pie like?"

"It's made with Saskatoon berries."

"What are Saskatoon berries?" I asked.

"They are little red berries that look like cranberries but are much sweeter," she explained.

"I'll have the tort," I said.

The waitress brought me a large piece of sponge cake filled with a pink strawberry-like fruit and topped with an artistic swirl of whipped cream. I cut through the corner of the cake and forked it into my mouth. Ummmmmmm! The taste was similar to fresh strawberry shortcake, only better. A beautiful city, great restaurant and delicious meal--life is good.

Early Tuesday morning while trying to air up my front tire I broke the stem of the tube and the tire went flat. Very few of my flat tires have been due to punctures, mostly rim problems, spoke-hole blowouts and stem problems. These skinny tubes are rather delicate.

The wind was to our backs pedaling out of Saskatoon on this sunny, warm morning. Northern Saskatchewan has a lot more trees than North Dakota or Southern Saskatchewan. In North Dakota it was necessary to search the horizon to find a single tree. North of Saskatoon trees appeared in all directions, including a forest stretching 30 or 40 miles along the South

Saskatchewan River Valley. We encountered a single big hill in a valley 20 miles north of Saskatoon. The bike's speedometer topped 32 mph flying down that hill.

It was time for a snack when we passed the Esso filling station in Longham. As Karen got off her bike, a beautiful, friendly tabby cat sauntered over and wove himself between her legs. He knew that Karen was a cat person. I snapped a photo as she knelt down to pet him.

Leaving the gas station we passed a farm where a big, determined pit bull dog charged out after us barking and snarling. We both shifted into high gear and pedaled for all we were worth. The dog wouldn't give up. He chased us for nearly two miles before he tired and turned back. Luckily we had a tail wind or he probably would have caught us.

"Do you want to stop and pet the nice doggy?" I asked Karen as he trotted back towards his farm.

"No, that's okay," Karen said as she caught her breath.

"It would make a good photo opportunity," I suggested. "I can see it now--Here is a picture of the dog biting Karen's leg! This picture is where the dog ripped Karen's bag off the bike and shredded it. Here's one where the dog is biting Karen's tire. See Karen's back tire go flat."

It was a perfect day for biking. The road was level and smooth, the weather warm and sunny, the wind to our back, the bikes were working well and we were in high spirits. Karen set the pace all day as we rode at 16-22 mph. Even with five rest stops, our average speed was an incredible 14 mph for 85 miles. That put us at the hotel in Battleford by 11:00 a.m., six hours after we left Saskatoon.

"What is there to see in Battleford?" I asked the desk clerk.

"The old fort has been reconstructed and it's very interesting," he replied.

After lunch, Karen and I biked five miles to Old Battleford and visited the local museum and Fort Battleford.

The NorthWest Mounted Police built the old log fort in 1876 when Battleford was made the capital of Canada's North West Territories. The detachment of 200 Mounties saw action during several skirmishes with the Cree Indians. Their successful battles led to the surrender of Chief Poundmaker and Big Bear, bringing peace and security to the area. Several of the homes and log buildings inside the fort were built in the late 1800s. By 1924, the mechanization of the Mounties made the fort unnecessary and it was closed. Later it was reopened as a Provincial Park.

After a tour of the fort, we biked back to the restaurant next to the motel for supper. I was feeling great when we left the restaurant--full belly, good conversation, interesting tour of the fort and pleasant weather. Then I spied a flat tire on my bike--flat number ten, another spoke blowout. That took the wind out of my sails. Karen rode her bike while I walked mine back to the motel. After the tire was changed, I tried to air the tube up and discovered that my portable tire pump wasn't working. A cold chill went down my back. What if the tire had gone flat on the road or over at Fort Battleford? The flat occurred near our motel, luckily. I borrowed Karen's bike and rode to Wal-Mart to buy a new tire pump and several more tubes. The Lord has been good to us. Our mechanical problems occurred in civilized locations where we could easily get help.

That evening, the radio station broadcasted a high-wind warning for the local area starting at midnight. During the night I could hear the wind howling as the weather front blew through. Wednesday morning dawned cold, cloudy and windy. Karen and I rode across the North Saskatchewan River and past Old Battleford at 10 mph with the wind growing stronger by the minute. Karen led for the first hour, allowing me to draft off of her. As the wind picked up, our speed slowed to 8 mph. Karen's back tire developed a slow leak and had to be pumped up hourly.

A 20-minute nap did wonders for my tired muscles.

Mid-morning we stopped to rest by a farm with a prairie museum. The big black labrador retriever that owned the farm came running out from the barn barking ferociously. He kept coming closer, barking and then backing away. Eventually he came up close enough to smell my hand. We were friends. Karen and I lay down in the tall grass, using the barn for a windbreak, and took a 20-minute nap.

Our speed dropped even lower as we pedaled on to Paynton against an ever-increasing wind. At Paynton, we stopped at a cafe for an egg sandwich. Fighting the fierce head wind was taking the fun out of biking. Karen decided that she didn't want to pedal another 50 miles to Lloydminster against that wind. I opted to go on. The Greyhound bus passed through Paynton and went on to Lloydminster so Karen planned to ride the bus to our motel.

"You'll have to box up the bike," the Greyhound agent told Karen. The attendant at the gas station started making Karen a bike box when a gentleman in a van who stopped for gas suggested he'd be glad to drive Karen to Lloydminster.

"I'm going that way anyhow," the fellow said as they loaded Karen's bike in the van.

Pedaling as hard as I could, my speed vacillated between 5 and 10 mph as the wind gusted and slacked off. To keep focused, it was necessary to set short-term, achievable goals. Every five miles I pulled over for a water and snack break, literally eating my way to Lloydminster. The wind was brutal. I kept waiting for it to die down--it never did. During the rest stops I consumed three candy bars, packages of peanuts, trail mix, Cheetos, Corn Nuts and a Dolly Madison cherry pie. I would have gained 10 pounds a week if it weren't for burning 5,000 calories a day pedaling. The wind seemed to gather more strength as the day went on. It was the kind that pushes the furniture off your porch, knocks over portable signs and blows the wash off the line. All I could do was put my head down, pedal and pray. Finally at 7:00 p.m. I biked into Lloydminster, 85 miles in 14 hours, 6 mph average. It was the longest biking day of my life and it turned out to be the most physical day of the entire trip.

Karen was reading alongside the pool when I checked in. She had arrived at 3:00 p.m., taken a shower and a nap before going to the pool. The hotel had a three-story water slide and Karen played on it while waiting for me to arrive. I immediately changed into my swimsuit and soaked my aching body in the hot tub for 30 minutes. There wasn't enough strength left in my legs to climb the three flights of stairs up to the water slide. Supper consisted of a 12 ounce T-bone steak, baked potato, peas, salad and cherry pie ala-mode. I went straight to bed, plumb tuckered out.

Thursday morning Karen and I woke refreshed from a good night's sleep and biked out of Lloydminster in bright sunshine. The slow leak in Karen's rear tire developed into a fast leak. It went from requiring air once an hour to every 15 minutes and then to every minute. We stopped at a Shell station in Vermilion to change it. A small thorn caused the leak--one of the few real punctures we encountered. Once the problem was taken care of, we ate a second breakfast of pancakes and maple syrup at the restaurant next to the service station.

A giant billboard outside of Vermilion showed a bare foot followed by "oeing." It was an eye-catching, clever ad. Karen and I discussed whether it was a garage advertising towing or a foot doctor advertising feet care. We decided that most likely it was a towing service.

From Vermilion we rode along at 15 to 20 mph with no wind. At Innisfree we rode up a steep hill to a truck stop and ate a delicious lunch of bacon and cheddar soup. From the dining room window we could see Birch Lake and the Provincial Bird Sanctuary in the distance. The surface of the huge lake shimmered in the noonday sun like a thousand stars. The temperature continued to climb as we pedaled along in the hot afternoon sun. Mid-afternoon we decided to stop for a 15-minute nap in the soft grass beside the road.

After 95 miles of fun biking, we pedaled into Vegreville and came face-to-face with the world's largest pysanka, a Ukrainian painted Easter egg. It weighs 5,000 pounds, is 25 feet long and 60 feet in diameter.

"Why an egg?" I asked. The answer was related in the history of the town.

Vegreville was first settled in the late 1800s when French farmers from Kansas arrived to cultivate the rich soils in the area. They named the settlement after their French Roman Catholic priest, Father Valentin Vegreville. At the turn of the century, Ukrainian settlers began to arrive in ever increasing numbers. Today, the town's 350 residents are predominantly Ukrainian.

At Vegreville we stopped to inspect the world's largest egg.

In 1973, the townspeople were discussing a project to put the town on the map. The 100th anniversary of the NorthWest Mounted Police, the forerunner of the Royal Canadian Mounted Police (RCMP), would occur in 1975. The Canadian government asked towns to submit proposals for monuments to commemorate the anniversary. The people of Vegreville decided to commemorate both the RCMP and their Ukrainian heritage by building a giant pysanka.

Archeologists discovered ceramic pysanky in the Ukraine dating back to 1300 B.C. Pysanka is derived from the verb "pysaty" (to write). The word literally means, "egg writing". Each color, line and design has a specific meaning. There are also egg rituals to bring good fortune and riches.

While chickens have been laying eggs for eons, Vegreville officials found that no one had ever described an egg mathematically. They hired Professor Ron Resch, a computer scientist at the University of Utah, and his team to tackle the task. Professor Resch's team spent 12,000 man-hours developing the computer program and manufacturing the individual aluminum panels for the egg. They prepared a design based on traditional pysanky principals and the town's people approved the gold, bronze and silver pattern.

The finished pysanka consisted of 3,500 individual aluminum triangles bolted together from the inside. The local gossip is that the worker who bolted the last piece together is still inside the egg. On July 28, 1975, the world's largest pysanka was dedicated.

"This Pysanka symbolizes the harmony, vitality and culture of the community and is dedicated as a tribute to the 100th anniversary of the Royal Canadian Mounted Police who brought peace and security to the largest multi-cultural settlement in all of Canada."

Vegreville is now on the map. Queen Elizabeth and Prince Phillip visited the pysanka in 1978. Each year thousands of visitors travel from all parts of the world for the annual Ukrainian Pysanka Festival in July. This is the sort of serendipity that makes the bike trip exciting and enjoyable.

Friday morning was cool and very windy as we left Vegreville, making it difficult to ride faster than 8 or 9 mph. On the edge of town was a monastery with a huge graveyard full of tall, white crosses. It looked like a war memorial, but turned out to be graves of the monks. We waved at an approaching train. The engineer played "Shave and a hair cut, two bits," on the train whistle and waved to return the greeting.

The continuous head wind turned the previous day's fun bike ride into a grueling grind. Mid-morning we stopped at an Esso station in Murdare to warm up with cups of hot chocolate. I needed to be at the airport in Edmonton at noon to meet grandson Paul's and daughter-in-law Connie's flight. At the rate we were going, we'd never make Edmonton by noon. It was time to ask for help. I called Perry Wiehart who runs Mundare Towing and he agreed to drive our bikes and us to Edmonton. Perry, who has a wife and four children, believes raising a family in a small town, like Mundare, can provide the Christian values and moral teachings that are missing in our big cities. He moved to Mundare from Vancouver Island, British Columbia when his grandmother left him a house in her will.

"We had to keep everything locked up in Vancouver Island or somebody would steal it," Perry said. "Here in Mundare, we leave the house and car unlocked. Everybody in town knows my kids and if they do something wrong, I'll hear about it before they come home."

Perry dropped us at the Best Western Motel in downtown Edmonton. Karen went to the pool while I caught the shuttle to the airport to meet Paul and Connie. At the airport, I stopped at the Hertz counter to rent the minivan Connie would drive up to Alaska.

"Do you really want to rent this van for a month?" the Hertz lady asked.

"Yes," I replied. "I'm biking to Alaska and my daughter-in-law is going to follow me up the Alaskan Highway in the van."

"I've never rented a van to anyone for a whole month. You know how much that is going to cost?"

"Yes, unfortunately I do," I replied as I handed her my credit card.

Paul and Connie's Northwest Airlines flight arrived right on time. They came out of customs and immigration each carrying a single sports bag. After hugs and kisses, I asked where their luggage was?

"You said pack light," Connie said. "This is all we brought."

We climbed into the van and drove to Wal-Mart to pick up supplies for the trip north: snacks, rain ponchos, drinks, picnic supplies, rope, mosquito repellant and a cooler. Then we drove to a bicycle shop and I bought two Kevlar bike tires. I had 3,000 miles on my tires and they were starting to show wear.

Back at the motel I contacted the manager and picked up the two mountain bikes and care packages Gloria shipped to the motel. My afternoon was spent assembling the bikes and sorting out the maps and bike parts. Karen, Connie and Paul took time to enjoy the motel's indoor pool.

After supper, I scanned the tourist information package in the motel room and read up on the city's history. Edmonton, the capital of Alberta, was founded in the late 1700s as the trading post Fort Edmonton, on the banks of the North Saskatchewan River. John Prudens, a Hudson Bay Company clerk, named the fort after his hometown Edmonton, England. In 1808, the original fort burned down and was rebuilt on the site of the present city.

Today, Edmonton is a big (650,000 population), busy city with too much traffic! After biking through the countryside for the past four weeks, Edmonton scared me. I felt very uncomfortable, even when driving the minivan.

On Saturday morning I hugged Karen as she caught the shuttle to the airport for her flight to Boulder.

"Did you enjoy the bike ride?" I asked.

"Yes," she replied. "But, like most things, it had its good points and bad points. I made up a list using the 'Harper's Index' format from Harper's Magazine."

Number of days biked: 6
Number of days of sunshine: 6
Total miles between Regina, SK, and Edmonton, AB: 500
Total miles I rode: 360
Average distance in miles planned per day: 85
Average number of stops made per day: 5

Average temperature at 5 a.m. when we started biking: 6C (42F)
Warmest afternoon temperature experienced: 22C (71F)
Number of days with headwinds: 3
Number of days that I had rides to the town we stayed: 3
Chance when I began each day's ride that I would finish: 50%
Average miles per hour traveled on the good days: 15
Average miles per hour against the wind: 6
Hours of biking it took on Tuesday to go 85 miles: 6
Hours of biking Wednesday to go 35 miles before I gave up: 7
Number of times I thought, "This isn't fun" (approx.): 429
Percentage of those thoughts occurred on Sunday, Wednesday,
    or Friday: 100%
Length in hours of my layover in Calgary: 5
Number of flights per day into Regina, SK: 3
Population of Regina, SK: 180,000
Conversion rate from U.S. to Canadian currency: 1.43
Number of hotels we stayed in with swimming pools, hot tubs
    and waterslides: 2
Number of dogs that chased us: 2
Number of goats that did: 1
Number of trucks carrying live chickens that passed us: 1
Number of grilled cheese sandwiches eaten at roadside diners: 6
Number of those that were consumed at 7:30 a.m.: 1
Distance in miles biked by 7:30 a.m. that day: 35
Length in feet of duct tape used to hold my bag on my bike after
    I lost my bungee cord: 4
Length of daylight in hours each day: 16
Number of flat tires changed: 2
Number of sheep that ran from us when we stopped by side of
    road (approx.): 20
Average number of cars and trucks that honked at us per day: 5
Number of trains that honked at us: 2
Distance in kilometers outside of towns that signs are placed to
    indicate services available in them: 1

Number of towns with a spinning wheel included on the
available services sign: 1
Number with a library indicated: 1
Number of channels in Saskatoon hotel carrying the
Avalanche/Stars hockey game: 4
Percentage of those that were in French: 50%
Average number of times per day we filled our water bottles
while riding: 2
Average number of glasses of water I drank at dinner: 7
Number of gears on the bike: 21
Average number used on a good day: 7
Average number used on a bad day: 18
Average number of people per stop who asked where we were
going: 1
Number of 60-foot diameter Ukrainian eggs seen: 1
Total hours it took Allen to bike to Lloydminster Wednesday: 14
Hours after I quit that Allen kept biking on Wednesday: 7.5
Number of movies I watched in that time: 1
Number of pages of my book read in that time: 127
Number of times I went down the three-story water slide in that
time: 5
Minutes spent in the hot tub in that time: 45
Number of days biking in Saskatchewan: 4
Number biking in Alberta: 2
Number of times daily that I applied sunscreen: 2
Number of body parts I sunburned anyway: 1
Length in minutes of my hot showers after a day's ride: 15
Number of times I thought about work: 2
Average seconds those thoughts stayed in my mind: 5
Number of mosquito bites: 4
Number of pictures taken: 49
Average distance in yards from hotel to restaurant where we ate
dinner: 30
Number of postcards I sent: 22
Average time of naps (minutes) taken after a day of riding: 135

Number of cats I petted at gas stations: 1
Weight in pounds of my bag: 10
Number of McDonald's I saw: 2
Number of Tim Hortons (a Canadian breakfast chain): 6
Number of other bikers encountered: 0
Years since I had seen my cousin, Paul: 13
Number of words Paul said to me in 18 hours (approx.): 25
Miles Allen still had to bike from Edmonton to the Arctic Circle:
      2,100
Number of days I ate Bran Flakes for breakfast: 3
Number of books read during the trip: 2
Ounces of trail mix eaten: 40
Number of times a Canadian ended a sentence with "eh?":
      Countless.

CHAPTER 7

GRANDSON PAUL'S FISHING TRIP

Paul agreed to bike the Alaskan Highway on one condition--that he could fish every day. I was willing to do whatever it took to get him to join me. One of the prime motivations for the adventures I undertake is to spend some quality time with my grandchildren.

Connie agreed to drive Paul and me to the edge of Edmonton. There was no way we were biking through the bumper-to-bumper, hectic traffic of downtown Edmonton. Our first problem was how to get four full-assembled bikes, snacks, cooler, luggage and three people in the van. We tied two bikes on the van roof, laid the back seat down and carefully maneuvered the two remaining bikes into the van first. Then we filled the remaining space with the luggage and cooler. Paul had to sit with his feet on a pile of luggage, but it was only a 15-minute ride. Connie let us out on the edge of town and we started biking along Trans-Canadian Highway 16. The weather was cold (40F) and partly cloudy with a light wind. At Manly Grove we turned north on Route 43, a smaller, less traveled road. The scenery changed from crowded civilization to open farm country as we transitioned to Route 43. Soon we saw the first signs of wilderness: forests of birch, poplar and spruce coming right down to the road.

Paul mastered the Cannondale's 21 gears quickly, smoothly shifting up and down as we rode over the hilly countryside. He was accustomed to riding an old Huffy ten-

Connie drove the support van while Allen and Paul biked.

speed with its hunt-and-seek gear shifter, and said the indexed gears on the Cannondale made shifting fun. He had not been biking much this spring and expected his youth and good physical condition would sustain him. For the past two months, he was working for a roofing contractor, carrying shingles up a ladder. Even with his lack of training, Paul kept up with me all morning.

Connie drove the support van and met us every 25 miles: Manly Corners, Glenevis and Mayerthorpe. It was a luxury having the van and meals on wheels! Snacks and a drink were waiting for us when we rode up. Connie would refill our water bottles and put a surprise snack in our backpack while we rested.

Paul started dropping behind me around mile 60. At our 70-mile snack stop, he opted to ride the remaining 25 miles in the van rather than bike it. For his first day, 70 miles was a significant accomplishment and a personal distance record. I was proud of him. Most people never complete a 70-mile bike ride in their entire lifetime.

The scenery in the afternoon gradually changed to thick forest, attractive lakes and crystal clear streams. In one valley, the road passed under a gigantic wooden, six-level-high railroad trestle that extended for a mile. It was straight out of the old western movies.

Most of the last 25 miles was uphill. I kept stopping to check if my tires were low or if something was wrong with the wheel bearing as I couldn't get the bike to go over 11 mph. Finally I realized that the road was going continuously up a gradual hill. When I finally reached the peak, a dark green forest stretched out below as far as the eye could see. It was like standing on the edge of the Grand Canyon. In the middle of the forest I spotted the tops of a few buildings and wisps of steam rising in the air--Whitecourt, Alberta. After drinking in this soul-satisfying scene, I cautiously started downhill. The road went down and down and down. I coasted down at 25 or 30 mph, alternately applying the front and rear brakes for the entire eight-mile run right into our motel parking lot. What a fantastic way to end the day--a long downhill run.

Fighting the fierce head winds the previous day into Edmonton with Karen had left me depressed, but the ride on Saturday lifted my spirits. It was the perfect end to a week of biking; good weather, light winds, interesting scenery, a long downhill finish and my grandson as a biking companion.

Sunday I biked out of Whitecourt at 5:00 a.m. on a frosty morning (32F) with a beautiful full moon setting in the west. The vapors rising from the river and the pink dawn sky created a surrealistic setting. The Alberta Newsprint Company plant belched huge clouds of steam, rising straight up to 1,000 feet and spreading out horizontally into a big anvil-head. The early-morning sun illuminated the cloud, but not the plant.

70

Grandson Paul, who biked 70 miles on Saturday, rode in the van Sunday because his knee was sore from a recent trampoline accident and the extensive exertion on Saturday.

I wore my long-sleeve biking shirt, a sweatshirt, jacket, biking shorts and biking gloves. My fingers, toes and legs were cold, but I generated enough heat pedaling to keep my body warm. The previous week Gloria sent me a hand-knitted headband to keep my ears from freezing and falling off. During the morning, I stopped every 20 or 30 minutes to stomp my feet and massage my hands to warm them. In planning the bike trip, I consciously chose the cold spring weather over the sweltering summer days and mosquitoes.

Outside of town I spotted a beaver's mud-and-stick house in a pond and a large, brown beaver swimming along with a mouthful of fresh branches. Deer appeared at the edge of the forest, grazing on the tender grass that grew by the road. Occasionally, one would dart across the road in front of me, bounding like a gazelle--so graceful. Ravens circled overhead and squirrels chattered from the nearby trees. I was finally in nature's backyard.

Construction contractors were adding the other two lanes of a divided highway. It was 5:00 a.m. Sunday morning, but already dozens of people were on the job. They have a very short road construction season in Alberta so they work 16-hour days, 7 days a week during the summer. I encountered three 10-mile long stretches of construction on my 100-mile ride this day. Lots of bulldozers, turnapuls, road graders, dump trucks and hundreds of construction workers.

Along the first 55 miles of highway out of Whitecourt, I encountered a wall-to-wall forest of pine and spruce. Not a single ranch, farm, house or cabin to be seen anywhere. What a beautiful stretch of wilderness! The lady at Little Smoky said it was Crown Land and no one could build there.

I encountered dozens of hills, but they were actually fun. With the slight tail wind, I could pedal uphill at 10-12 mph and

71

zoom down at 25-30 mph. Our luggage was riding in the van with Connie so the bike was very lightly loaded.

She stopped at Fox Lake so Paul could fish. While he was getting into position, he slipped off a log and fell in the lake. To add insult to injury, he didn't even get a bite.

Connie and Paul had a snack waiting for me at a general store in the village of Little Smoky, named for the Little Smoky River. The owner of the store asked where we were biking from.

"Dayton, Ohio," I told her.

"I've been there," she said, her eyes twinkling with excitement. "I flew to Cincinnati so often that it was like my second home. My son was badly burned when he was three years old. We flew him to the Shriner's Hospital for Children in Cincinnati on a regular basis from then until he was 18. I loved going to Kings Island Amusement Park. Some older ladies told me where to sit on each ride to get the biggest thrill."

"How long since you've been to Cincinnati?" I asked.

"About five years now. My son doesn't need to go back to the hospital any more."

"Looks like your cat is about to burst," I said as a very pregnant black cat walked through the store.

"Yeah, Smug is due any day now. You wouldn't like to take a kitten along, would you?" the lady asked with a laugh.

"I love kittens, but I think the ride might be a little much for a new born. I see you have Saskatoon Berry ice cream. I'll have a single dip cone."

The ice cream was creamy, fruity and delicious.

Paul fished in Little Smoky River and caught a 12-inch-long pike and a big kingfish using a minnow lure. He had forgotten to bring his fishing knife on the trip so he bought a neat Buck knife in the general store.

Full of ice cream and good cheer, I biked on to Valleyview, Alberta, which sits on top of a big hill. The last 25 miles were mostly uphill. The day's 110-mile ride took nine hours for an average speed of 12 mph--a great day of biking.

72

The sky clouded up in the late afternoon and the wind started howling. Cold chills ran down my back as I listened to the wind and thought about the tough ride Karen and I had pedaled across the Saskatchewan plains.

At 5:00 a.m. Monday morning, I encountered a deer grazing alongside the road at the edge of town and another one bound across the road about ten miles later. All together I encountered eight deer that day. They were mule deer, stockier than the white-tail deer in Ohio and they have a very broad rear end. Paul decided his knee needed another day of rest so he rode in the van. Besides, it is a scientifically proven fact that teenagers are not totally functional at 5:00 a.m. It was unreasonable to expect him to bike at that ungodly time of day.

I kept gaining altitude, building up potential energy, as the uphill runs were longer than the downhill ones. Finally, I reached the top of the plateau and started down into the Smoky River Valley, converting all the potential energy I'd stored in the past hour into kinetic energy (energy of motion). Riding down into the 600-foot deep valley I reached a top speed of 37 mph before I crossed the Smoky River, a large, fast-flowing body of water. Six rivers (Smoky, Red Willow, Beaver Lodge, Wapiti, Bear and Simonette) and a dozen creeks join together within five miles upstream from the bridge to convert the peaceful Smoky into a raging torrent. The sides of the valley are sheer cliffs where the floodwaters have eroded the rock away. The Smoky River flows north, emptying into the Peace River about 100 miles north of the bridge and eventually into Hudson Bay.

A strong head wind developed mid-morning as I biked into Bezanson. A big, shaggy good-natured sheep dog ran out of a farmyard and loped alongside my bike for the last mile into the village. He decided to cross the road just as a big truck came barreling by. The truck driver slammed on his brakes and swerved--the tires screeched--he missed the dog. The noise scared me so much I ran off the road and fell into the ditch.

73

Paul, Connie and the sheep dog were waiting for me at the truck stop after I extracted the bike from the muddy ditch. We ate a snack and then Paul biked with me the rest of the way to Grande Prairie. Fortunately, we only had about 20 miles to go, riding at 9 or 10 mph against the head wind. We stopped to read the tourist information sign at Kleskom Hills, a prehistoric river delta along the same strata as the Cretaceous dinosaur bed at Drumheller. Geologists have found some unique dinosaurs at Drumheller, which are now exhibited at the Museum of Man in Ottawa. Then we continued on to Grande Prairie, which used to be at the bottom of an ancient shallow sea. Our motel was called the Igloo Inn. No, it was not made out of blocks of ice, just a plain wood-frame building.

The moon appeared big and bright as I biked solo out of Grande Prairie on Tuesday morning. The snow-covered Canadian Rocky Mountains unfolded 100 miles to the south when I crested the first hill outside of town. The snow appeared pink in the dawn's light.

At noon I biked across the British Columbia border and stopped for a snack with Connie and Paul. British Columbia must work on a limited tourist advertising budget. Their "Welcome to British Columbia" sign is small compared to Alberta's sign across the road. I pedaled into Dawson Creek, Mile Zero for the Alaskan Highway about 1:30 p.m. They are in the Pacific Time Zone so we gained another hour. These 25-hour days are great, enough time to catch up with ourselves.

Connie and I walked up to the tourist center to learn a little about Dawson Creek's history. George Mercer Dawson was a Canadian government geologist commissioned to survey the border from Minnesota to the Pacific Ocean as part of the North American Boundary Commission. In 1875 and again in 1879, he was in the Dawson Creek area in connection with the commission and a subsequent survey to find the best route for the Canadian National Railroad. The local creek was named for him, as was the town when it developed. In March of 1942,

Dawson Creek was a quiet town of 600 farmers, trappers, hunters and railroad workers. Because it was the northern end of the rail line, the U.S. Army Corp of Engineers decided to use it as the starting point for the Alaskan Highway, Mile Zero. That month, 6,000 soldiers and 600 flatbed rail cars of construction equipment arrived in Dawson Creek. For the next three years, men and equipment passed through the town on the way to build, upgrade and maintain the highway.

At the end of the war, tourists started driving up the highway to Alaska. Motels, gas stations, restaurants and tourist shops opened to service them. Today, Dawson Creek is no longer a sleepy little town. It supports a year-round population of 11,150, has 15 motels, 45 restaurants, 13 gas stations, 10 souvenir shops and 21 churches.

CHAPTER 8

THE CHALLENGE OF BUILDING THE ALASKAN HIGHWAY

I have dreamed of traveling the Alaskan Highway for 50 years. Finally I was there, Dawson Creek and Mile Zero. I've pieced together the following account of the building of the highway from interviews with people who worked it, books and videos.

"When I first flew into Whitehorse, Yukon in 1943, I was astounded by the enormous engineering challenge the Army undertook to build the Alaskan Highway," retired Army Colonel Ed Austin of Centerville, Ohio told me. "I was in charge of the 33 dentists who were stationed at the remote camps up and down the highway. During the year I was there, I traveled the entire length of the highway four times using anything that would move--trucks, jeeps, planes, half-tracks, caterpillars, boats and dogsleds. A couple of times we got caught out in blizzards so bad we stopped dead in our tracks. To keep from freezing to death in the minus 70 degree temperatures, I put one sleeping bag inside another, crawled in and covered my head. I saw firsthand the difficult conditions the workers suffered through to build and maintain that road."

Why did they build the highway? Soon after the purchase of Alaska from the Russians in 1867, business, government and civil groups began requesting a land route to the new territory. With the discovery of gold in the Klondike in 1896, the demands for construction of a trail, road or railroad

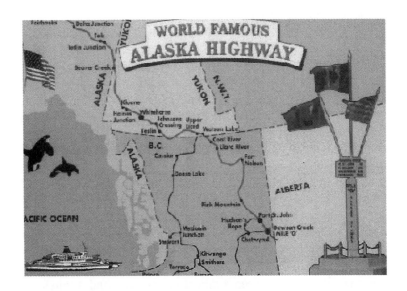

We finally reached the Alaskan Highway at Dawson Creek.

intensified. However, with only a few thousand permanent residents in Alaska, the tremendous construction costs could not be justified. In 1928, a group of Alaskan businessmen, lead by Donald MacDonald, again proposed a road and completed a 450-mile preliminary survey (Kakm Video, 1995). To attract attention to the proposal, MacDonald hired Slim Williams in 1933 to travel the proposed route on his dogsled. It took Williams 5 months to dogsled the 2,200-mile route between Fairbanks and Seattle, Washington. While the stunt received extensive press coverage, it did not move the U.S. government to action. In 1939 Williams repeated the trip on a motorcycle in six months. Again no government response was forthcoming. It would take something much bigger to jar money from the federal treasury for a road to Alaska.

The bombing of Pearl Harbor on December 7, 1941 was the kind of event necessary to loosen the purse strings. The only supply route to Alaska was the Pacific Ocean sea-lanes from the West Coast. With most of the U.S. Pacific fleet in flames, the security of that route was in jeopardy. Plans for a land route to Alaska were underway in early 1942 when the Japanese attacked and captured two of Alaska's Aleutian Islands, Attu and Kiska. The cold reality that the Japanese occupation of those islands invoked was best expressed by George Murray, a Canadian reporter for the Ottawa Evening Newspaper: "We will either build a highway up to Alaska or the Japanese will build it down for us!"

On February 14, 1942, the directive was finally issued to start work on a road from the railhead at Dawson Creek, British Columbia, to Delta Junction, Alaska, where it intersected the existing Richardson Highway to Fairbanks (Cohen, 1979). The route would follow the Northwest Staging Route, a string of airbases carved out of the wilderness by the Canadians to support an airmail route between Edmonton, Alberta and Whitehorse, Yukon. The orders directed the Army to "push a pioneer road to Alaska with all possible speed."

To speed up construction, simultaneous efforts were started from Dawson Creek north, from Ft. Nelson north, from Whitehorse both north and south, and from Delta Junction, Alaska south. Bulldozers, road graders, steamrollers and trucks were loaded on rail cars and cargo ships destined for Alaska and Canada. In one five-week period, 600 boxcars of equipment and supplies arrived at the tiny village of Dawson Creek, British Columbia, population 200.

The lack of skilled heavy-equipment operators was a serious problem (Lundberg, 1999). The commander of the field engineers complained, "We've got millions of dollars of brand-new heavy equipment and a bunch of grocery clerks, fruit pickers, seamen, cowpunchers and school teachers to run it!"

The Army shipped 11,000 officers and men to Alaska and Canada for the road building effort. Congress directed the Public Road Administration (PRA) to hire private contractors to assist the Army. The PRA hired five management companies and assigned each a section of the highway. The management companies hired 81 contractor companies who employed 14,000 men on the highway crews.

The Army engineers had little experience with construction in an Arctic environment. They had to learn as they went. When the road builders first encountered the muskeg, a thick layer of decayed vegetation, the engineers dug it up and shoved it to the side. The men soon learned that when uncovered, the permanently frozen ground underneath, permafrost, turned to a muddy soup that could swallow a huge bulldozer or truck. After their initial mistakes, the engineers learned to cover the muskeg with brush and gravel to insulate the permafrost. Bridges built over the narrow, active channels in the mile-wide glacier riverbeds soon became bridges over a dry creek bed since the channels changed rapidly. The active channel would dry up in a month and a new channel would open up half a mile away.

The road, which followed trapper's trails, streambeds and animal trails, was far from straight. One rumor suggested that the road was purposely built with curves to prevent Japanese planes from landing their airplanes on it. One 32-mile stretch from Prophet River to the Jackfish River had an incredible 135 curves. People joked that the Army Corp of Engineers used that stretch to practice building curves.

The military and civilian road builders lived in tents that had to be moved every few days since the road was being built at the incredible pace of five miles per day. Living in a tent with winter temperatures dropping below minus 50F required considerable fortitude and ingenuity. However, many of the workers preferred that to fighting the hordes of mosquitoes, black flies and no-see-ums (small gnats) in the summer. Huge mosquitoes that were able to penetrate the thick hide of a moose and drain a quart of blood from the animal per day, loved to attack the thousands of thin-skinned bipeds who were trying to drive a bulldozer, chop down a tree or eat their lunch. As many as 6,000 mosquitoes were counted simultaneously drawing blood from one caribou. One harried worker commented, "If the Japanese invaded and occupied this forsaken country, it would serve them right!"

"As an officer assigned to Headquarters in Whitehorse, I lived in a log cabin which was a considerable improvement over the Quonset huts and tents the enlisted men and civilians lived in," Colonel Austin said. "The Army didn't have an adequate supply of cold-weather clothing and initially issued rubber boots for Arctic wear. The men quickly learned those boots didn't keep their feet warm. Where possible the men bought native mukluks. I watched the native women chewing the caribou or reindeer hide to soften it for the mukluks."

The weather was only one of the dangers the men had to cope with. A group of workers were bathing in a Yukon stream when a bear attacked them. They escaped by punching the bear in the snout and swimming away underwater. Bears were a constant threat in the remote camps, especially around the cook tents and garbage dumps. The problem was so bad in one camp that the commander posted a sign: "If chased by a bear, don't run into camp!"

It took a lot of ingenuity and courage to build the road through the wilderness. Every day the road builders encountered new challenges. The following is an account by Heath Twichell (Twichell, 1992) of building the road along the southern end of Muncho Lake, the most expensive section of the entire highway.

"The cliff ran sheer down to the water line, but below this the action of the waves and ice had cut holes, some big enough to hold a box of TNT. Lt Mike Miletich of the 35th Engineers sent a man up the cliff to fasten a long rope to a protruding rock. Then Miletich took his clothes off, fastened the rope under his arms and dove into the icy lake. Using the rope for support, he explored the face of the cliff until he located an underwater hole the right size. After swimming back and getting a box of TNT, he swam out to the cliff face and placed the TNT in the underwater hole. He made one more trip to shore where he rigged a stick of dynamite with a blasting cap and a waterproof fuse. Lt Miletich lit the fuse, put the explosive between his teeth and swam back to the hole with the fuse sputtering and set to go off at the proper time. He stuck the dynamite in the box of TNT and swam out of danger before the thing blew up, (Twichell, 1992)."

Colonel Austin described other problems the workers faced in the remote environment.

"Our dental clinics along the highway were as basic as the workers living conditions. We had the Army's standard 'Chest-60' dental kit at each of the remote clinics. It consisted of a footlocker filled with basic dental instruments and a foot engine connected through a long revolving shaft to power the drill. The dentist, or his assistant, pumped the foot pedal to keep the drill turning. Our patients were not happy with the pain inflicted by operation of that primitive drill. I eventually was able to procure electric motors for the drills."

Feeding a moving army of workers proved to be a real challenge. Often the cooks substituted fresh-killed moose or caribou in place of the dried or canned meats sent up from the Army Depots. Fresh eggs were impossible to obtain. The workmen complained bitterly about the awful taste of the powdered eggs. One camp kept a young moose named Velvet as a mascot. Velvet sneaked into the mess tent one day and ate five pounds of powdered eggs before anyone noticed. Within 24 hours, Velvet got sick and died, adding credence to the claim that the powdered eggs were inedible.

On October 25, 1942 at Beaver Creek, Yukon, the 18th Engineers working down from Delta Junction met the 97th Engineers working up from Whitehorse, completing the 1,671-mile long Alaskan Highway in an incredible 256 days. Because of the secrecy order imposed on the road builders, no public announcement of the completion was made that day. However, within 24 hours, the Japanese broadcast the completion of the road.

It is hard to appreciate the total magnitude of the effort, but some numbers associated with the project provide a clue, (Dziuban, 1959):

11,000 military troops
14,000 civilian workers
11,000 pieces of road-building equipment
100,000 barrels of fuel
133 bridges
8,000 culverts
$135 million cost ($80,000 per mile)
1,671 miles long
minus 70F winter temperature
256 days to complete highway (average 6.5 miles/day)
4,000 tons of dynamite
1 billion mosquitoes

The combined force of military engineers and civilian contractors successfully completed the greatest engineering challenge since the building of the Panama Canal in one season and opened access to the most beautiful wilderness areas in the world.

CHAPTER 9

THE ALASKAN HIGHWAY WAS EVERYTHING I HOPED IT WOULD BE

A red fox with a white-tipped tail dashed across the road as I pedaled out to Dawson Creek on the famous Alaskan Highway. I stopped the bike and whipped out my camera as it ran up the hill. It stopped at the top, sat on a stump and posed. After I took the photo, the fox trotted back down towards me and posed for two more photos. A mule deer bounded out of the brush and crossed the road a few miles out of town. The highway started as perfectly smooth asphalt at Dawson Creek and changed to dimpled asphalt with small cracks around the ten-mile marker as I biked along the six-foot wide shoulder. Paul's knee was still bothering him so he elected to ride in the van.

Turning off the new road at mile marker 18, I proceeded down the old Alaskan Highway three miles to the Kiskatinaw River Bridge, the only original wooden bridge still used along the Alaskan Highway. The old road consisted of bumpy asphalt with several gravel sections giving me an idea of what the original road was like in 1943 when it was first completed. The bridge is a beautiful 200-foot long, 100-foot high trestle that curves nine degrees as it crosses the deep canyon cut by the Kiskatinaw River. It was built in 1943 from massive timbers of British Columbian black spruce and was still in very good repair. Biking across the deserted wooden bridge I could picture the

The only wooden (1943) Alaskan Highway bridge still in use.

feverish activity along the road during the war, with trucks speeding much-needed supplies to Alaska.

Paul climbed down the steep, gravel bank to the river and fished while I took photos of the bridge from a dozen different angles. He caught a good-sized bottom-feeding fish, possibly a sturgeon. It was a cold morning and the river was covered in fog when we first arrived. The morning sun warmed the air and dispersed the fog by the time we finished taking photos. After eating a roast beef sandwich, I followed the cut-off road leading back to the new highway.

Coasting down a steep, foggy hill into the Peace River Valley, I crossed the Peace River Bridge 40 miles north of Dawson Creek. This is the longest bridge along the Alaskan Highway and from my perspective on the bicycle, it looked as though it went on forever. A few miles later I pedaled through the edge of Ft. St. John. Motels and fast-food restaurants

Paul (circled) fishing under the trestle bridge.

occupied every corner, cluttering the road and generating too much automobile traffic.

Connie, Paul and I ate lunch at a rest stop at Charlies Lake. A tourist information sign explained the history of the village. Before the arrival of the U.S., troops in 1942, Charlies Lake was a quiet community of homesteaders and trappers. In the spring of 1942, 6,000 soldiers arrived there to set up camp. Many people consider Charlies Lake, Mile Marker 52, the real start of the Alaskan Highway since there already was a primitive road from Dawson Creek to Charlies Lake when it was decided to build the highway to Alaska. One of the worst construction disasters occurred at Charlies Lake. To transport workers and equipment north and bypass crews already staggered along the route, portable pontoon-bridge sections were used to cover 11 kilometers of water from the south end of the lake to Stodderts Creek in the north. A number of the pontoon sections were joined together at the south end of the lake and barged across the

Paul caught a nice-sized fish in the Kiskatinaw River.

lake to extend the already built section. One day in May 1942, four soldiers refused to board the barge because of high winds and rough water. They were immediately arrested and put in the brig for insubordination. As the barge rounded the point where the golf course is today, crosswinds and high waves flooded the sections and the barge broke up, dumping the workers into the icy waters.

A lone trapper, who witnessed the disaster from his cabin, rushed to his rowboat to aid the victims. A number of workers clung to the sides of his boat and were saved. Three bodies washed up on the shore several days later. The trapper received a medal for his bravery and the arrested soldiers were released.

A 25-foot high Paul Bunyan statue greeted me as I biked past a lumber mill a few miles north of Charlies Lake. The lumber mill used the statue as an attention-getting advertisement.

I stopped for a snack and a photo. Babe, Paul Bunyan's big blue ox, was nowhere in sight.

I had very few problems with bugs or mosquitoes on the trip thus far. Apparently it was still cold enough that the main mosquito crop hadn't hatched. When I rode through Minnesota, I ran into a few clouds of small black bugs, but they didn't chase me. In Saskatchewan, Karen received a couple of mosquito bites when we stopped for a snack by a lake, but again no big problem. She also ran into a bug as she was zooming down one of the hills and it splattered on her sunglasses like they do on a car's windshield.

The Shepherd's Inn appeared on the horizon about 1:00 p.m. completing my first day's 72-mile ride along the Alaskan Highway in 8 hours, a comfortable 9 mph average. As I registered, I asked the manager, Harold Witner, how long he'd been in British Columbia?

"I came to British Columbia in 1972 with a group of people from Pennsylvania to start a Christian Community," Harold replied.

The Christian Community intrigued me so after parking the bike in my room, I walked back to the office/restaurant and spent two hours talking to him and his wife, Geraldine, about the Christian Community over a pot of tea.

"About 700 or 800 people came up here in the early 70s," Harold explained. "We homesteaded six communities around here, mostly farming communities. The Shepherd's Inn community has about 160 people. An elder council governs each of the independent communities. We're not affiliated with any specific church; we're more a combination of religions to fit our needs. We came to British Columbia to prepare a refuge for God's people. Today, with all our modern conveniences, people are busier than ever. In the olden days, the farmer used a horse to pull the plow. It could only work an eight hours a day so the farmer only plowed for eight hours. Farmers are now working longer hours using a tractor that will run all day. They have to pay for their equipment and modern conveniences. We live a slower, simpler life up here."

"Do you feel safer in your Christian Community?" I asked.

"Only God can make you safe. It's not other people I need to worry about harming me; I have to find safety in God," Harold told me.

"Have you always worked at a motel or store up here?"

"No," Harold replied with a smile. "I've done about everything--farming, construction, store keeping and running a trap line. For two years I trapped martin, wolves, lynx, beaver and wolverine. Wolverines are the cleverest animal of all. One time, three wolverines tore up eight miles of my sets. They turned my unsprung traps over and ate the martins that were caught. It's impossible to catch a smart wolverine in a spring trap so I built a house (box) trap and baited it with meat. Caught two of the wolverines and never heard from the third one again. Trapping was a real challenge, a challenge from within."

"Do you have TV?"

"No, we don't receive TV here. We not only object to the program content, but to the time robbing aspect of it. We do have some TV sets that are used to watch video tapes."

"Is your community aging? Do the youngsters move away?"

"No, I don't think so," Harold replied. "A number of our youngsters work in St. Johns, but live here. The same characteristics that make them good Christians gives them a good work ethic and makes them reliable workers. My son is a minister in the Four Square ministry founded by Aimee McPherison."

"That's interesting," I said. "My Uncle Donald Grant was a minister in the Four Square ministry back in the 1930s."

Harold's wife, Geraldine, joined us. She was born and raised in Ludlow, Massachusetts. After her husband died, she moved to an Alaskan Christian Community with her children

88

and mother. She met Harold when his son married her daughter. They were both widowed and eventually decided to marry. Geraldine has three grandchildren. Her mother, Louise Almelda (age 74) and two of her grandchildren also joined us.

"Are the children home schooled?" I asked.

"Yes," Geraldine said. "There aren't enough children in the community to support a public school."

During this bike trip, I've observed that when I talk with people in small communities their primary goal is to raise their children with good moral standards and a good work ethic. Making money appears to be the goal for people I meet from the cities.

Paul, Connie and I ate supper at Shepherd's Inn, hamburger-vegetable soup; spaghetti; two-inch-thick, hot, home-baked bread and cherry cheesecake for desert. When I asked for the bill, the waitress told us the meal was compliments of the management (Harold and Geraldine).

Just past the Shepherd's Inn, I saw a sign to the historic Beatton River Flight Strip, one of four gravel airstrips used as emergency landing strips for aircraft travelling the Northwest Staging Route to Alaska. In the early 1940s, the Canadian government built a series of landing strips from Edmonton, Alberta to Alaska. Over 8,000 aircraft, mostly short-range fighters, flew to Alaska and then on to Russia as part of our Lend-Lease program. Many of the fighters landed at Beatton River for fuel, repairs or to avoid bad weather. The airstrip was closed after the war.

On Thursday, I discovered there was no level road between Shepherd's Inn and Pink Mountain, only hills. I spent the entire day pedaling up at 6-10 mph and coasting down at 25-30 mph. As I pedaled up one hill, a pickup truck stopped and the driver, Patrick, asked how far I was biking. He is a marathon runner and president of the running club in Grande Prairie, Alberta. He plans to organize a running relay from Dawson

Creek to Ft. Nelson. We talked about training techniques, goals and the Alaskan Highway.

Mid-day I biked into the village of Wonowon, which I assumed was the Indian name for "blueberry patch on top of the hill where many brown bears live." I stopped to read the "Point of Interest" sign and learned that Wonowon was originally Blueberry Control Gate, an Army checkpoint on the Alaskan Highway. During the war, the Army allowed only official-business vehicles through the checkpoint, as it was strictly a military road. After the war, when the Army turned the checkpoint over to the Canadian government, the locals named the surrounding town Wonowon because it was at milepost "one-o-one."

The majestic, snow-covered Canadian Rocky Mountains rose in the west as I biked out of Wonowon. Thirty miles up the road I passed the cutoff that used to go down "Suicide Hill." This hill was the steepest grade on the entire highway until they bypassed it in the 1960s for safety reasons. I'd seen pictures of the road sign announcing the approach to the hill--PREPARE TO MEET THY MAKER!

By the time I reached Pink Mountain, the Rockies wrapped around three sides of the horizon. The only direction not hemmed in by the majestic mountains was to the east. I biked into the motel at 11:30 a.m., completing the 70 miles in 6.5 hours in spite of all the hills.

"What shall we do this afternoon?" I asked Connie and Paul.

"The lady in the gift shop said there is a spectacular waterfall up the road," Connie said. "She suggested we drive up there to see it."

We walked back to the gift shop and asked directions.

"Drive north about 15 miles and turn left on a gravel oil pipeline road towards Grassy Oil Fields. Follow the gravel road about ten miles to a picnic area. Then you have to walk about

Canadian Rocky Mountains, forest and Sikanni River Falls.

two miles through the woods to get to the falls," the shopkeeper told us.

We followed her detailed directions and found the picnic area. After parking we walked through a thick spruce forest toward the river. The roar of the waterfall could be heard a mile away. Finally, the path started downhill and we found ourselves at the edge of a 600-foot deep canyon. There, through the spruce trees, we caught the breathtaking view of Sikanni Falls. To get a better view, we needed to climb down the sheer sides of the canyon.

"Do you want to go down?" I asked Connie.

"I didn't come this far just to hear the falls," she said.

Paul located some ropes tied to a tree at the top of the canyon. The three of us started repelling, hand-over-hand, down the canyon walls. The ropes stretched down to a narrow shelf 200 feet above the river. Very carefully, Paul and I scooted over

Paul and Connie enjoying the view at Sikanni Falls.

to the edge of the shelf and came face-to-face with a panorama of rushing water and sheer canyon walls. Connie, who has a fear of heights, clutched onto the tree branches for support. Millions of gallons of snowmelt water from the Rockies roared through the narrow cut in the rock cliffs, creating a rainbow as it splashed on the boulders 200 feet below. A thick sheet of ice hung over the protected north wall of the canyon indicating a substantial spring lay above the wall. We sat for a long time transfixed by the power and remoteness of the waterfall. I doubt that one tourist group a day takes the trouble to witness this spectacular sight.

"Do we have to go back up the same way we came down?" Connie asked.

"We could jump in the river and float down to the bridge," I suggested. "As a matter of fact, this river flows north.

We could float to Fort Nelson and then all the way to the Arctic Ocean."

"Ahhhh, no thanks," Paul said looking at the raging torrent below us.

Using the rope we slowly worked our way up the side of the canyon, stopping at each tree to rest. Thirty minutes later all three of us reached the top of the canyon wall.

"The lady said there are some dinosaur bones along the canyon wall above the falls," Paul said. "Can we go looking for them?"

"I don't think so," I replied. "Not unless we have a better idea where they are. We could search for a week if we don't know where to look. This is pretty rough terrain."

A baby caribou grazed alongside the road as we headed back to Pink Mountain. Connie stopped the van so I could take a photo. As I rolled down my window, it stopped nibbling on the tender grass, raised its head and posed. After posing, it resumed eating. A mile down the highway we passed the mama caribou frantically searching for her baby.

The Alaskan Highway became so rough for the last ten miles into Pink Mountain on Thursday that I had trouble focusing my eyes while riding the high-pressure, skinny-tired road bike. Friday morning we switched to the low-pressure, fat-tired mountain bikes that Gloria had shipped to Canada. These were much more comfortable to ride as Paul and I pedaled out of Pink Mountain at 5:00 a.m. on a cold (40F), sunny morning. The road started at 3,600 feet, not far below the highest point on the Alaskan Highway, and went down and up all day. Flat road is at a premium along this stretch of the highway. The wind felt cold riding downhill but we warmed up pedaling uphill. The road leading down to Sikanni River was the steepest we've ever biked, a nine-percent grade for two miles. We flew down the hill at 35 mph, very fast for our mountain bikes. Mid-day Paul's knee started to ache so he rode in the van. When I stopped to remove my jacket, a moose and her calf wandered out of the woods 100 feet away and walked towards me. I grabbed my camera and started taking photos.

She reminded me of the nearsighted Mr. Magoo in the cartoons. She would walk ten feet towards me, then stop and appear to squint to see what kind of animal I was. Then she would walk another ten feet, stop and look again. She and her calf came within 50 feet of me when a car appeared in the distance. The moose looked at the car, trotted across the road and disappeared into the woods. How close would she have come if the car hadn't driven by?

It was early afternoon when I biked into Prophet River, completing the 83-mile ride in 9 hours. That wasn't bad for the first day on the mountain bike, but the increased road-resistance wore me out. I was in bed by 7:30 p.m.

I felt revived after a good night's sleep. The morning dawned cool (40F) and cloudy with a light rain. The old highway from Prophet River had an unbelievable 132 curves in the 35-mile stretch to Jackfish River. An anonymous poet asked the question: "Were the guys who built this road going to Hell or coming back?" The curvy section was replaced in 1992 with a straighter road.

The rain steadily increased until it turned into a downpour around 7:00 a.m. The fog rolled in and visibility dropped to less than one mile. I wore my Gore-Tex jacket and pants with my rain poncho over the top. It was hard to build up any enthusiasm when my glasses were spotted with rain and visibility limited to the roadside ditches. I set short-term goals to keep my mind off pedaling since there wasn't much scenery. Every ten miles I stopped for a snack and a drink of water. The rain continued for the entire day with the temperature hovering between 40F and 45F.

I stopped at the Trapper's Den on the outskirts of Ft. Nelson, a souvenir shop in a real log cabin. They offered a large collection of furs, antlers, hides and items made from them. The owner, John Wells, is a trapper and traps most of the furs he sells. One of the furs I was particularly interested in was the British Columbian pine martin. When I was 15 years old, I trapped muskrats back in Illinois. Martin was one of the most valuable wild animal pelts at that time. I decided I would move to British Columbia after high school and trap martin for a living. During my junior year, I drew the plans for a log cabin and searched through the Sears-Roebuck catalog, making a list of everything needed to furnish it. College took precedence over trapping, but I never forgot the year I spent dreaming about trapping martin. I bought a martin pelt from John so I could show my grandchildren what my dream was about.

Leaving the Trapper's Den, I pedaled across the Muskwa ("bear" in Indian) River, the lowest point on the Alaskan Highway, and up the hill into Ft. Nelson. After registering at the Travel Lodge, I jumped in the hot tub to soak away my aches and pains. Ahhhhhhhh, that felt good! The soak and a shower made me feel human again. Ft. Nelson has a great tourist museum with displays of local history, highway history and stuffed animals. Paul, Connie and I drove to the museum and watched a movie about the building of the highway. We learned that Fort Nelson was established in 1805 as a fur trading post and named for British Admiral Horatio Nelson who died that year at the battle of Trafalgar. Today, the town has a population of 5,500.

The Alaskan Highway was everything I hoped it would be. I have traveled along some of the original highway, encountered wild animals every day (moose, caribou, deer, fox, rabbits and ermines), ridden through endless forests with the snow-covered Canadian Rocky Mountains in view, and talked to dozens of interesting people.

Part of my expectations about the highway came from the description my dear friend, Mrs. Marge Oliver, related to me. She and her husband, Jack, drove up the highway in the early 1960s when it was still very primitive.

"My husband and I liked to travel and in 1963 we started talking about driving to Alaska," Marge said. "Jack worked at Dayton Tire and when his boss heard we were thinking of driving up the Alaskan Highway, he arranged for Dayton Tire to loan us six tires to test for them. That was all the push we needed to settle on the trip.

"We loaded a cooler, camp stove and some blankets in our Chevy and headed up through Montana into Canada. Our route was up through Canada to Dawson Creek, British Columbia and then up the Alaskan Highway to Whitehorse, Yukon. We stopped at campgrounds, sometimes renting a cabin and other times just sleeping out. I remember one night we slept on a picnic table.

"The road from Dawson Creek was gravel and rough. When we saw a mail truck coming, we just pulled over to the side and let them pass. They threw gravel all over and made a cloud of dust that took minutes to settle. We never had any car problems or blowouts, but we sure got a lot of paint nicks from the flying gravel.

"Around Whitehorse we took a side trip to see a gold mine. Jack was driving down this rough gravel road when it quit abruptly at the edge of the river. He got out and saw a hand-lettered sign nailed to a tree. It said to push the button to call the ferry. I thought it was a joke, but Jack pushed the button and a few minutes later a ferry appeared and took us across the river. We toured the gold mine and then tried our hand at gold panning. I got a few flakes of gold out of the sand, but I got my fanny wet in the process.

"We drove back to Whitehorse and then continued up the highway to Alaska. Jack suggested we stop at a diner at Dot Lake, Alaska for pie and coffee. We started talking to the man and woman who owned the restaurant and they invited us to spend the night with them. That evening, the couple took us to a nearby Indian village. One of the Indian dancers was wearing a headdress made with caribou antlers. I mentioned how pretty the headdress was and the Indian gave it to me. One of my daughters has it now. Those people were all so friendly, they never charged us for staying with them or for anything. Matter of fact, everyone we met on the trip was pleasant.

"When we got down around Anchorage, we saw the salmon swimming up river. That was a sight I'll never forget, giant salmon fighting their way up those white-water streams.

"What was the prettiest part of the trip?" I asked.

"Well, every day I had to screw my eyeballs back in their sockets," Marge said. "I'd think, 'Boy it can't get any prettier than this,' and the next day the scenery would be even more spectacular, more beautiful. If I didn't have three daughters at home to take care of, I would have just stayed up there. I love to collect rocks and crystals, and we had the car full of them when we drove home. Most of them turned out to be white quartz. Alaska was the prettiest place I've ever been," Marge said.

CHAPTER 10
SUMMIT--THE HIGHEST POINT

The strong smell of wood smoke hung in the air as I stepped out of the motel Monday morning. I looked up the street and saw a huge cloud of smoke rising near the edge of town. As I biked up to the scene, 20 firefighters manned the hoses and sprayed water on a still-burning building as gigantic clouds of steam billowed skyward. It was burnt clear down to the ground! Yellow tongues of flame licked at the few smoldering pieces of the walls still standing.

"What happened?" I asked one of the firemen, who happened to be a woman.

"They had a party in the Trapper's Pub last night," the lady replied. "I guess it was a pretty hot blast!"

The 100-year-old Trap-Line Hotel, the oldest hotel in Ft. Nelson, and Trapper's Pub were totally destroyed. Fire claims a lot of the old, wooden structures in these northern towns. If the buildings don't catch fire internally, then a forest fire often burned up to the edge of town and showers everything with glowing embers.

A gentle rain fell as I left the scene and biked out of Ft. Nelson. My batteries, both physical and mental, were fully recharged after a relaxing day off, Sunday. I felt great, though a little apprehensive. The hotel clerk advised me that it was snowing in the mountains both north and south of Ft. Nelson. Ft. Nelson was the lowest point on the Alaskan Highway, 1,000 feet above sea level. This day I planned to bike to the highest point on the Alaskan Highway, Summit, at 4,200 feet. The 3,200-foot climb promised to be a significant challenge made even more interesting with rain and snow.

The gradual slope of the road allowed me to ride at 12-13 mph. Outside of town a large, brown deer leapt out of the woods and ran along the road beside me. It kept up for a mile, then stopped, looked at me as if to say, "Is that the fastest you can go?" and bounded into the woods at twice the speed I was biking.

Halfway to Steamboat, the road started abruptly uphill and continued to become steeper and steeper as I approached the village. Steamboat takes its name from nearby Steamboat Mountain, which from the scenic viewing point resembles a paddle-wheel steamboat. I stopped to rest by a small stream with a beaver dam and a big mound-shaped beaver house constructed of small limbs and mud. Continuing on in the cold rain, I was huffing and puffing clouds of steam by the time I reached Steamboat, the midpoint on the way to Summit. The village consists solely of a gas station/restaurant/residence. A young boy rollerbladed across the wooden front porch as I biked up. Connie and Paul met me in the restaurant parking lot.

"Not much room to rollerblade up here," I said when I walked in the restaurant.

"No," replied the owner, Ed Paynter. "We don't have any paved sidewalks or streets here except the highway and we don't let my son skate there."

"How long have you run the restaurant?" I asked.

"My wife, Carol, and I started coming up here from Fort St. John five years ago to run the restaurant during the summer. I think this year we're going to stay through the winter. It'll be tough because the weather gets pretty bad and there isn't much traffic or business during the off season."

"Can I get a bowl of soup?" I asked.

"I've got a pot of homemade chicken noodle soup on the stove now," Carol said. "It'll be ready in a minute. How about some hot, home-baked bread while you wait?"

I sat down close to the glowing pot-bellied wood stove to dry out and warm up. Ed brought us a platter of delicious hot bread and I wolfed down three thick slices covered with real butter. Carol brought more bread with the soup. I ate two bowls of soup, three more slices of bread and a piece of homemade cherry pie ala mode for dessert. Biking up those hills burned a lot of calories and I needed to refuel often. These delicious home-cooked meals not only provided the required nourishment, but also supplied a much-needed psychological boost to my spirits. While pedaling uphill in the cold rain, the dream of sitting by a roaring fire and eating a hot, delicious meal sustained me.

While we ate, Ed entertained us with tales about the mountains, the forest, homesteading, bush pilots and the Alaskan Highway.

"Any problems with bears up here?" I asked.

"Just last week while I was driving up the road, I noticed a biker ahead. A bear ran out of the woods and started chasing the fellow. The biker was pedaling uphill for all he was worth, but the bear continued to gain on him. I blew my horn and scared it away."

"I've never seen a burl as big as the one you have out front," I said, referring to the ten-foot high section of a giant white spruce tree in Ed's parking lot with a burl four-feet in diameter.

"I found that burl down in the valley when I was hunting one year. Couple of summers ago I cut it down and hauled it up here. Darn thing turned out to be a witching burl. When we first moved up here, I dug several wells to get water for the restaurant and none produced much quantity. They would go dry every time we flushed the toilet. While digging the hole to set that burl in, we found the old Army water well from 1942. After cleaning the well out, it has never gone dry."

"What causes the burl to form?"

The snow was five-inches deep in the mountain pass.

"It's a virus that attacks the tree. The virus causes an imbalance in the chemicals that control growth and the tree's growth mechanism goes wild. The burl forms around the attacked area in just a year or two. It is sort of like a cancerous tumor, but it doesn't seem to hurt the tree."

Warm, dry, well fed and entertained, I started biking uphill from Steamboat through the area where Ed saved the biker from the bear. Connie and Paul drove right behind me and we all kept a sharp lookout for that crazy bear. Fortunately, the bear failed to appear.

The rain continued and the temperature dropped as we gained altitude. I stopped at the next pass, stared through the hazy clouds and could just barely make out Indian Head Mountain, a high crag resembling an Indian's profile. The rain finally turned to wet snow, with 5 inches of accumulation on the

The Alaskan Highway deteriorated to gravel potholes.

ground by the time I biked over a pass at the 3,000-foot level. The mountain bike was equipped with knobby tires so I was able to slip and slide my way through the snow. A few miles later, the road deteriorated to gravel and potholes for a distance of ten miles. The big trucks and RVs threw mud all over me as they whizzed by. My shoes, legs, pants, bike, jacket and face were completely covered with yellow mud.

The snow turned to rain in the late afternoon, which washed some of the mud off me. I passed a number of mountain streams that were still covered with ice and snow. The rushing melt-water of the streams was gradually carving openings in the ice-cover.

I was exhausted when I finally reached Summit Lake. The 89-mile ride and 3,200-foot climb took 11.5 hours. Connie and Paul were off fishing in the frigid waters of Summit Lake when I arrived. My first priority was to hose the mud off my bike and then I turned the water on me. Second priority was a hot, soothing soak in the bathtub. Ahhhhh, that felt wonderful.

Third priority was supper. I especially looked forward to the fresh-baked bread, homemade soups and unique homemade desserts these little restaurants offered. This night, supper consisted of hamburger steak, chicken-rice soup and steamed vegetables. For dessert I had two helpings of warm banana-nut bread with butter and a big glass of cold milk.

After supper, Connie, Paul and I drove a few miles down the road to the Erosion Pillars. These are 50-foot-high cones of granite that stick up after the softer limestone material eroded away. Standing by the pillars we had a spectacular view of the forested hills, the snowcapped-mountains and water from the streams tumbling down into the MacDonald River Valley far below us.

After our scenic tour, I retired to the motel room to complete my daily chores: oil the bike, clean the chain, check the tire pressure and tighten all the bolts. With the equipment taken care of, my attention turned to typing my daily notes into the computer and studying the topographic maps along the next day's route.

The temperature stood at 30 degrees with a mixture of rain and snow Tuesday morning as we started out of Summit at dawn, 4:00 a.m. A mountain sheep appeared along the edge of the road and stood silhouetted against the snowy sky. Photo op. As I took several photos, the sheep walked nonchalantly up the road and passed me, 15 feet away, on the other side. A man on a bicycle apparently didn't seem like a threat to him.

At Summit Lake, I stopped to look at the crystal-clear lake that was still half covered with ice. Paul caught his first-ever trout in the lake the previous night. Just past the lake, the highway started downhill. I alternately applied the front and rear brakes, as it became steeper and steeper. The road was too wet and slippery to take full advantage of the downhill run. The view of the distant mountains, the crashing streams and the green

Paul and Allen never walked up any of the steep hills.

valley below was breathtaking as I coasted around the sharp
mountain curves and down into the valley. Dozens of mountain
sheep grazed on the hillsides just off the road. Once in the
valley, my route was along a fast-flowing, rocky stream full of
snowmelt water.

Toad River, British Columbia, established in 1941, was
the only settlement I passed through in the valley. The village
consisted of a dozen houses and a couple of business buildings,
but no restaurant or gas station. It might be hard to convince my
wife to live in a town called Toad River. The name conjures up
an unpleasant image--toads hopping out of the river and invading
the house. A few miles past Toad River, I encountered a
beautiful rainbow, which led me to Folded Mountain at mile
marker 428. The information sign there explained that originally
all the limestone lay flat on a shallow seabed of the western
continental shelf, where it had accumulated grain-by-grain for

over a billion years. About 175 million years ago, the continent of North America began to move westward, overriding the Pacific Ocean floor and colliding with offshore chains of islands. The continental shelf was caught in a squeeze. The flat-lying layers slowly buckled into z-shaped folds, like I saw there.

After a few hours of enjoying the level terrain, I started up a mountain at the other side of the valley. The climb up the 3,000-foot high pass to Muncho Lake proved even more physically demanding than the previous day's ride to Summit. It was steeper and longer. I biked the eight-miles long hill in low gear at four mph, and stopped to rest halfway up. There was no grass at the side of the road so I sat on my folded sweatshirt while eating a snack. Then I packed up and rode off with my sweatshirt still lying by the side of the road.

I finally caught up with Connie and Paul at Muncho Lake. Connie and I ate lunch at a wooded rest stop while Paul fished. She was getting some cookies out of the back of the van when something big and hairy appeared on the wooded hill 30 feet away.

"Bear!" Connie yelled. She dropped the cookies, jumped in the van and rolled up the windows.

The "bear" turned out to be the gray, fuzzy rear-end of a grazing mule deer. Connie's yell startled the poor deer. It looked around at us with huge, wild eyes and then bounded off into the woods.

Muncho Lake is one of the most beautiful areas we visited. The lake is crystal clear, calm, long (7 miles), narrow (1 mile), deep (300 feet) and surrounded by snow-covered mountains. The small community there is equipped to host thousands of campers, hikers, mountain climbers, fishermen, hunters and sightseers. The area was uninhabited until the Alaskan Highway was built. The road snaking along the lake's rocky eastern shore proved to be the most expensive section of highway to build. Horse-drawn barges were used to haul away

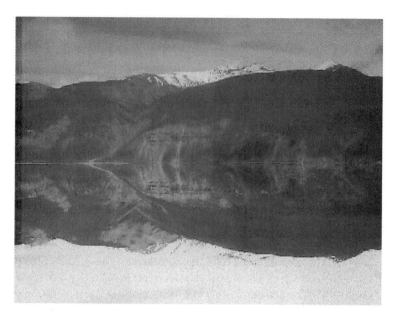

Glassy smooth Muncho Lake reflected the mountains.

the excavated rock dynamited loose from the steep shore. During construction, a lot of machinery and equipment was lost over the edges of rocky ledges into the 300-foot deep lake. After the highway was completed, the Signal Corp and Northwest Service Command built a maintenance camp at Muncho Lake to service the highway and telephone cables.

Today, the lodge at Muncho Lake is a beautiful, three-story, log building with all the charm and conveniences of a resort hotel. It has a cathedral ceiling and a big fireplace in the lobby. The staff can arrange boat tours of the lake or floatplane tours of the area, which leave right from the lodge's dock.

Small herds of mountain sheep grazed and played alongside the road as I biked along the lake. The young sheep jumped around, butting and chasing each other. That day I counted over 30 sheep.

106

The road between Muncho Lake and Liard River was under construction. They were straightening many of the curves and making the grades more gradual. The current hills along that road were very steep. The speedometer on my bike registered 39 mph while flying down one of the hills. At Liard River, I rode across the only suspension bridge on the Alaskan Highway. That 1943 bridge is still in good repair.

At the Liard River Inn, Connie, Paul and I enjoyed a delightful supper while watching the chipmunks and birds competing for the seeds at the bird feeder outside the dining room window. The hotel's gray cat, Mouser, curled up at my feet during supper. I left the only sweatshirt I brought on the trip sitting alongside the road near Muncho Lake so I bought a Liard River sweatshirt with an Indian design from the hotel's gift shop to replace it.

A mile up the road from the Inn is Liard River Hot Springs, the second largest hot springs in Canada. Hunters and trappers told legends of the hot springs for several hundred years. They claimed there was a tropical paradise where exotic animals roamed and a garden of jungle-like greenery that survived the harsh winters. In 1942, when the Alaskan Highway was built through the area, the construction team cut a trail to the springs and found acres of lush, tropical giant ostrich ferns, cow parsnip, sundew, butterwort and aquatic bladderwort growing among the hot springs. The crews used the hot springs daily, with Sunday being reserved for the women in the camp. Today, there is a campground and parking area along the highway with a mile-long boardwalk leading back through the lush spruce marsh to the main hot springs. Over 250 species of boreal forest plants, 28 different mammals and 104 species of birds live in this area, many surviving only because of the warm, moist micro-climate created by the springs. The ferns, swamp plants and flowers reminded me of wandering through Audubon Swamp at Magnolia Plantation outside of Charleston, South Carolina, except I didn't see any alligators here.

107

The sparkling-clear spring water bubbles out of the ground at about 118F. It has a high mineral content and slight sulfur smell. At one end of the 100-foot long main pool, the hot water bubbles up while at the other end a cool spring flows in. By picking my spot between the merging temperatures, I could relax in water at a temperature varying from 70F to 118F. Soaking in the hot mineral water soothed my sore, tired muscles and almost put me to sleep.

CHAPTER 11

FLYING THE NORTHWEST STAGING ROUTE

Mouser, the hotel's gray cat, walked into my room when I opened the door early Wednesday morning. She jumped up on my bed and snuggled down in a fold of the covers. I scratched her ears and belly while she purred so loudly I thought she would wake Connie across the hall. Mouser followed me into the bathroom and played with a drip in the bathtub while I washed in the sink. Then she scampered back to my room and fell asleep on the bed.

Ground fog crept along the river and covered parts of the mountains as I biked out of Liard River. Around Liard Hot Springs, a pungent sulpher odor permeated the air. An adult black bear walked out of the woods about a mile from the hot springs and ambled along the edge of the roadside clearing looking for breakfast. I stopped and snapped a flash-photo. The bear stood up on its hind legs and squinted at me. We both stood absolutely still, about 300 feet apart, assessing the situation. Slowly, I climbed on my bike and started riding toward the bear to see if I could get a closer photo. No way! It turned and hightailed into the woods. No killer-bear encounter today.

A little further on I passed a dozen buffalo grazing by the side of the highway. There were several bulls, three or four cows and six calves in a tight circle. The calves were frolicking in the cool morning air, butting each other and running into the adults. The herd didn't move when cars stopped and people got

109

out to photograph them. The bulls would look up, acknowledge the people and then put their heads down and continue eating. No wonder they were nearly shot into extinction back in the late 1800s. The Canadian woodland buffalo are slightly larger than our American plains buffalo. The bulls grow to 2,000 to 2,500 pounds. Buffalo meat is available in the local stores. It tastes like high-grade beef and a single bull carcass can provide up to 700 pounds of boned-out meat.

The temperature hung a few degrees above freezing in the early morning and the damp fog sent a chill through me. I stopped periodically to soak up some warmth from the brilliant sunshine. The road was relatively flat following the Liard River Valley. I had ridden out of the Canadian Rockies.

Between Liard River and Fireside I passed a sign pointing off to the Smith River Airfield. In the late 1930s, the U.S. government worked with the Canadian government to establish a series of airfields from Edmonton, Alberta, to Fairbanks, Alaska. Smith River Airfield was one of these remote landing strips on the way to Alaska. The airfield particularly intrigued me since the previous day I had received an interesting e-mail from a friend back in Dayton.

"Reading your fantastic progress reports with great interest," retired Air Force Major Robert Van Trees e-mailed me. "Way back in the spring of 1943 I was flying P-39s from Great Falls, Montana, to Fairbanks and well remember the stretch from Dawson Creek to Fairbanks. We called it 'the aluminum highway' because of the number of aircraft that crashed along that stretch. At Whitehorse I always took a deep breath and said to myself 'only 525 more miles'!"

How did it happen that a string of good airfields existed across Northwest Canada between Edmonton and Whitehorse even before the Alaskan Highway was built? Since the early 1920s, the bush pilots had been pioneering airways in the Canadian Northwest. In 1924, a flight of four U.S. Army De Havilland "4's" flew from Edmonton through Whitehorse to

110

Alaska, (Dziuban, 1959). The early round-the-world flight by Wiley Post in 1930 followed the direct route from Fairbanks to Edmonton. Surveys by the Canadian Postal Service in 1935 concluded that the air route through Ft. Nelson and Watson Lake was not only the shortest route to Whitehorse, "but the climatic conditions and terrain were more favourable," (Wilson, 1943).

Weekly airmail service was instituted in 1937 between Edmonton and Whitehorse via Ft. Nelson and Watson Lake. By 1939, all-weather airfields were under construction at Grande Prairie, Ft. St. John, Ft. Nelson, Watson Lake and Whitehorse. After the bombing of Pearl Harbor, the U.S. decided to send a squadron of aircraft up the Northwest Staging Route to bolster Alaska's limited defenses. In February 1942, twenty-five P-40s and thirteen B-26s were dispatched to Fairbanks. A month later, only thirteen P-40s and eight B-26s had arrived safely at Ladd Field. Five more P-40s were grounded enroute and the rest (seven P-40s and five B-26s) had crashed along the way. The bad showing was blamed on the poor training for flying in the winter weather conditions encountered and the limited alternate airfields. The Canadian government had already established radio navigation aids every 200 miles along the route, but the airfields that existed only provided for austere operations. If they were going to fly large numbers of aircraft to Alaska, the U.S. and Canada agreed additional airfields must be built along the route and the facilities at the existing airfields enlarged.

The decision to supply Russia with lend-lease aircraft via the Alaska-Siberia route rather than over the North Pole or via Greenland dictated that large-scale improvements to the Northwest Staging Route must begin immediately, (Standley, 1945). By early 1943, the U.S. was moving 440 aircraft a month up the Northwest Staging Route with minimal losses. The new airfields built at Dawson Creek, Sikanni Chief River, Prophet River, Liard River, Pine Lake, Squanga River, Smith River, Pon Lake, Teslin, Snag and Burwash Landing provided a landing opportunity every 100 miles and helped carry the increased number of aircraft arrivals. During one week in August 1943, the airfields along the Northwest Staging Route successfully handled over 2,500 aircraft arrivals.

Having the aircraft fly up the Alaskan Highway provided the pilots with the prospect of a quick recovery if they were forced to crash-land. If they could walk out to the road, they had a high probability of being picked up quickly due to the constant traffic along the highway, (Baker, 1943).

Over 8,600 aircraft were flown up the Northwest Staging Route to Alaska during the war years. Of these, 7,930 were lend-lease fighter aircraft destined for Russia. While most of the U.S. ferry pilots were recent graduates of pilot training with no combat experience, the Russian pilots who picked up the aircraft in Fairbanks were seasoned combat veterans. The Russians considered flying 5,000 miles across the frozen Siberian wilderness to be a reward and vacation for their best combat pilots. The story is told of a new 2nd Lieutenant airfield officer at Ladd Field reading out a Russian pilot who had just landed there, (Ford & MacBain, 1944).

"You didn't use proper tower communications procedures on your approach, you came in too low and you cut the base leg short," the 2nd Lt said. "What kind of a pilot are you?"

The Russian pilot looked the airfield officer straight in the eye and replied, "I shoot down 12 Nazi planes. You?"

While in Alaska, the Russian pilots stocked up on items that were unavailable at home, like chocolates, Coca-Cola, nylons, perfume and female underwear. After leaving Ladd Field, the Russians refueled at Nome before heading across Siberia. Without spare parts and with a limited supply of high-octane aviation fuel in Siberia, flying 5,000 miles across the frozen wasteland often proved as dangerous as combat.

After I completed my bike ride to Alaska and returned to Dayton, I visited Major Van Trees to learn the rest of his story.

"When I completed basic training in February 1943, I was assigned to the 2nd Ferry Group of the Ferry Command at New Castle AFB in Wilmington, Delaware," Major Van Trees said. "My first mission was flying copilot on a B-17 to Scotland. In May 1943, my commander told me and three other pilots to pick up P-39s at the Bell Aircraft factory in Buffalo, New York, and fly them to Fairbanks, Alaska. Our flight leader had made several previous trips to Alaska and was familiar with the route. We flew from Buffalo through Illinois to St. Louis, Missouri; Oklahoma City, Oklahoma; Great Falls, Montana; Calgary, British Columbia; Edmonton, Alberta; Dawson Creek; Ft. Nelson, British Columbia; Whitehorse, Yukon and finally Ladd Field near Fairbanks, Alaska. We followed the Alaskan Highway as a navigation aid and to be near a road if we had to crash land."

"Did you have any problems with bad weather?" I asked

"No, we only flew in CAVU weather--ceiling and visibility unlimited. If we encountered snow or rain, we just parked and waited it out. We flew 500 to 2,000 feet above the terrain so we were under the clouds most of the time."

"How many trips did you make to Alaska?"

"I flew three trips up the Northwest Staging Route between May and July 1943."

"Did you have any aircraft problems or support problems?"

"No, my flights were routine. We flew the P-39 at about 250 mph and we carried 2 or 3 hours worth of fuel so we generally flew 500-mile legs. We did lose a lot of aircraft along the route, but my trips were trouble free. When we got to Alaska, we delivered the fighters and caught a hop back home on a C-47. The cargo aircraft were hauling freight to Alaska and hauling people back home. It was beautiful flying over the unbroken wilderness of the Yukon," Major Van Trees recalled.

I left Smith River Airfield and by mid-morning was in Fireside, stopping at Dora's Café for a steaming bowl of homemade chicken noodle soup. Bev and her husband sold their charter-bus business in Calgary 11 years ago, moved to Fireside and built the restaurant which they named after Bev's mother, Dora. The restaurant is open only four months a year, mid-May through mid-September because the diesel fuel for the electric generator costs $2,000/month and there isn't enough winter traffic to pay for the fuel. They recently completed a 12-unit motel--each room with a different color scheme.

"The rooms are more like guest rooms in your home," Bev said. "The towels, sheets and accessories are all matched to the wall colors. The blue room has blue seashell decorations in the bathroom, the yellow room has daisies. All the rooms have real paintings costing $500 and more. We have shampoo, lotion and toothpaste in the bath. We even provide two miniature bottles of Amaretto liqueur and a complimentary breakfast."

That's very fancy for northern British Columbia where most motel rooms are eight feet by ten feet with clapboard walls and a bath down the hall.

The sounds of the wild entertained me as I biked out of Fireside: the wind rustling through the leaves, water splashing down the hillside, the crows cawing and the birds singing---very pleasant.

Late in the afternoon I encountered three men cutting trees and bulldozing the shoulders on a sharp curve. I stopped for a snack and started talking to one of the workers.

"I'm Vern Hinson," the fellow said as he extended his huge, callused workman's hand for a handshake. "My boys and I have the contract to clear this curve so they can straighten it out. I own Iron Creek Lodge just up the road."

"That's where I'm headed," I replied. "I noticed the mosquitoes don't bother you even though you've got your sleeves rolled up. They're eating me alive! What's the secret?"

"They just don't like me much, I guess," Vern said. "I've gotten immune to their bites so it doesn't itch if they do bite me."

114

"How long have you lived here?"

"We moved here from Northern Alberta about ten years ago and bought the lodge. I like running the lodge and meeting the people, but my boys don't want any part of it. They prefer working in the woods."

I left Vern and biked on to Iron Creek Lodge, arriving about 4:00 p.m. The lodge consists of a barn-shaped building with a restaurant on the first floor, Vern's living quarters upstairs and a big lake in the back. An eight-unit motel is set off to the side.

We ate a delicious supper of roast beef and mashed potatoes on the lodge's screened-in back porch while a mama moose and her yearling calf swam across the lake behind the lodge. Vern said they get in the water primarily to get away from the mosquitoes and flies. After supper Connie, Paul and I took a restful canoe ride on the crystal-clear lake. As we glided along the placid water, the only sounds heard were from the wilderness--the whistling of the wind, frogs croaking, the splash of a fish jumping and a couple of moose crashing through the forest. The warm, golden rays from the evening sun danced on the sparkling water. We could see foot-long trout in the water so Paul tried fishing there. No luck, the trout swam right by his bait.

We left the Canadian Rocky Mountains to the south at Liard River on Wednesday and Thursday rode into the snow-covered Mackenzie Mountain Range to the north. The mountains appeared far away in the morning, but by evening we were at the foot of those snow-capped peaks.

Mosquitoes became a serious problem, swarming out of the woods and attacking us when we stopped to rest. On Thursday, the black flies joined them. The little black flies bit our ears until they bled. The black flies and mosquitoes couldn't catch us when we were riding, only when we stopped.

I biked across the Yukon border and stopped to photograph the "Welcome to the Yukon" sign. The first village I encountered in the Yukon was Watson Lake, eight miles from the border. The village had its beginning at the end of the nineteenth century. When word of the Klondike gold rush reached the outside world, American Frank Watson from Lake Tahoe left Edmonton, Alberta, and headed up the wilderness trail to the Yukon gold fields. After struggling for almost a year over the rugged, unmapped terrain, he found himself on the banks of the upper Liard River in the spring of 1898. Exhausted from traveling the difficult trail and realizing that all the good claims would be taken before he arrived, Frank decided to stop and try his luck in the beautiful valley where he found himself. He built a cabin on a lake that would later be named for him. There he hunted, trapped and prospected.

In 1941, other people moved into the Watson Lake area when the Canadian government started construction of an airfield there as part of the Northwest Staging Route. In 1942, the population of Watson Lake exploded as the U.S. government set up an accommodation and supply center for that section of the Alaskan Highway. With the end of the war, Watson Lake became a key transportation, communications and distribution center for the mining and logging industry in southern Yukon and northern British Columbia. With its current population of 1,600, Watson Lake is the third largest town in the Yukon, behind Whitehorse and Dawson City. It has also become a major tourist center and the Yukon Gateway for anyone, like me, who was traveling up from the south.

Today, Watson Lake's business district is a five-mile strip of motels, restaurants, tire shops, auto repair shops, gift shops, grocery stores, banks and gas stations spread along the highway. The traffic is horrible. Connie met me in town and we visited the famous signpost forest. When the Alaskan Highway was built in 1942, a homesick U.S. Army GI named Carl Lindsey from Danville, Illinois, erected a sign pointing the direction and giving mileage to his hometown. Others followed his lead and now there are over 34,000 signs in Watson Lake's world-famous signpost forest.   Connie talked to Henriette Devrie, who runs the sign-painting stand.   She donated a free sign to our bike trip, which I used to advertise one of my sponsors, the Sumner Press of Sumner, Illinois.

The road deteriorated to gravel for the first ten miles out of Watson Lake. I choked on dust for an hour from the heavy local traffic. The dust became so thick it coated my glasses. The big trucks and RVs also threw up gravel, stinging my legs as they roared past a few feet from my bicycle. I was continually moving over to the deep-graveled shoulder to get away from the flying rocks. Riding in the deep gravel took twice as much effort as riding on asphalt. By the end of the 75-mile, 8.5-hour day, I was tired and covered with dust.

Friday, we saw a gray wolf and a gray fox loping along the edge of the woods near Big Creek Recreation Center.   I watched the wolf carefully, not sure whether it was dangerous or not. It was apparently looking for lunch. It just ran along the edge of the woods, exploring every dead tree and culvert. When we stopped for lunch at Rancheria, the man at the gas pumps said a wolf was chasing bikers about seven miles north of the motel. I biked away from the motel with Connie driving the van right behind me for the first ten miles. It worked, the wolf didn't appear.

For the past two day's our route followed the Liard River upstream. This day we crossed the Continental Divide 20 miles north of Rancheria. The rivers on the east side of the divide flow northeast to the Liard and Mackenzie Rivers, then into the Arctic Ocean. The rivers on the west side of the divide flow southwest to the Gulf of Alaska. During the afternoon, I started biking downhill beside the Swift River.

On Saturday, I continued down-stream along the Swift River on a perfect biking day: 48F, sunny, calm and a good road. I rode at 15-17 mph slightly downhill most of the day with a few small uphill runs. The snow-capped mountains surrounded me.   The colors and shadows on the mountains changed throughout the day. In the morning, the snow looked pink in the dawn sun. At noon it turned white and by evening it appeared golden.

I met my first biker today, Bruce from Anchorage. Bruce is a college student at the University of Alaska and an avid biker. He was heading across Canada on a summer holiday, biking about 50 miles a day and camping out. His idea of a biking holiday was to sleep until noon, bike until evening and then party or visit until early morning. He told me a German and a Swiss biker were also headed east. I passed them a few minutes later. They each had 70 to100 pounds of gear on their bikes as they pedaled uphill very slowly.

Connie, Paul and I stopped for the day in Teslin at the Yukon Motel. Teslin, which means long, skinny water in the Tlingit Indian language, was originally the summer home of the Indians from coastal Alaska and British Columbia. A permanent settlement sprung up around 1903 when a trading post was established to trade with the nomadic Indians. Today, the village's 500 residents operate the resorts, campgrounds and tourist-related industries.

Paul fished in the bay behind the motel that afternoon. Using a minnow-lure, he caught a five-pound pike on his first cast. He has been fishing since he was two years old and that northern pike was the biggest fish he has ever caught. He was grinning from ear-to-ear when he showed us the fish. For Paul, it made all the biking effort worthwhile.

We ate supper at Mukluk Annie's Salmon Bake on the outskirts of Teslin on Saturday night. Paul ordered steak as usual, but Connie and I went for the fresh salmon. The huge slabs of fish were slow-cooked on a big grill over a wood fire. The baked salmon had a slight wood-smoked flavor and melted in my mouth. It was by far, the best salmon I have ever eaten. Oh, the joys of finding a great, new restaurant. Unfortunately, it's a 3,000-mile drive from Dayton.

118

Each day I biked through the beautiful unbroken wilderness.

This had been a fantastic week of biking through the splendors of northern British Columbia and southern Yukon. It is hard to find enough descriptive words to do justice to the endless virgin forests with no visible roads, countless wild animals, snow-capped mountains, sparkling lakes and cascading streams. You have to experience the wilderness to believe it.

Sunday dawned cool, cloudy and calm, a perfect day. Grandson, Paul, flew home to Missouri with memories of his big fish and my last biking partner, Karla Reichert, an occupational therapist from Dayton, flew to Alaska.

A deer bounded along the edge of the woods as I started biking from Johnson's Corner. The road was generally flat and level as I rode at 13-15 mph most of the day. Speaking of days, we were so far north that we enjoyed 21 hours of daylight. It was only dark from midnight until 3:00 a.m. I biked across the 138th longitude today, 800 miles west of Los Angeles.

I often encountered deer in the early morning.

Approaching Whitehorse, I encountered dozens of Sunday bikers. It was embarrassing when the young ladies would zoom past me on the uphill stretches. I thought I was riding pretty fast, but they were going faster. I arrived at the High Country Inn in Whitehorse at 12:30 p.m., 79 miles in less than 7 hours, a great day. Whitehorse is the capital as well as the biggest city in the Yukon. We were back in civilization: Pizza Hut, McDonalds, Kentucky Fried Chicken, Subway and telephones.

Whitehorse didn't even exist until a hundred years ago. In 1897, gold miners heading for the Klondike landed at Skagway, climbed Chilkoot Pass and sailed down a chain of lakes to the Yukon River. A treacherous stretch of rapids and foaming white water on the Yukon was nicknamed White Horse Rapids by the local Indians because it resembled the flowing mane of a white horse. Miners had to unload their boats and portage their supplies around the White Horse Rapids until some enterprising men built a tramway to bypass the rapids. In 1900, the White Pass and Yukon Railroad was built from Skagway to a point just beyond the White Horse Rapids. The new town at the railhead took its name from the famous rapids and Whitehorse was born. Riverboats met the trains and transported people and supplies down the Yukon to Dawson City and other gold mining towns.

As the gold strikes declined in the Klondike, Dawson City's population and importance also dwindled. Whitehorse saw a small but steady increase in population until 1942 when its population exploded as hordes of soldiers and civilians poured in to build the Yukon section of the Alaskan Highway. By 1950, Whitehorse celebrated the fact that it had the largest population in the Yukon by incorporating itself as a city. In 1953, the Yukon Territory capital was transferred from Dawson City to Whitehorse. Today, the bustling, modern capital has a population of 24,000, two-thirds of the total population of the entire Territory. Nestled between the mountains, surrounded by the forest and built on the Yukon River, Whitehorse is a clean, modern city with all the comforts of a metropolitan area.

Connie and I went sightseeing at the Old Log Anglican Church built in 1900 by Reverend Richard Bowen to minister to the Yukon prospectors. Bishop Isaac Stringer, who often preached at the Log Church, set out for Dawson City in 1909 and ran into an Arctic blizzard. He and his companion had only three day's provisions on a trip that eventually took them three weeks. Determined to survive, Bishop Stringer boiled his extra pair of seal-skin boots which had whale-skin soles, and toasted them over the fire. He ate the tops first, then the soles and the middles last. He reported the soles were the best part. (This was the origin of Charlie Chaplin's famous scene in his "Klondike" silent movie where he ate his boots). The Bishop and his partner eventually stumbled into an Indian village where they were fed and helped back to Whitehorse. Isaac Stringer was known from

The Klondike Steamboat plied the Yukon River for 50 years.

then on as the Bishop who ate his boots. The log church was active until 1960 when a modern church replaced it.

We also visited the S.S. Klondike, a large paddlewheel steam ship on display by the Yukon River. For almost 100 years, the sternwheeler was the mainstay of the Yukon transportation system. During the late 1800s and early 1900s, 250 paddlewheel ships moved passengers, freight and ore up and down the Yukon River and its tributaries. This was the only practical mode of transportation in a rugged land. The Klondike was built in Whitehorse in 1929 and she represented a breakthrough in sternwheeler design. Her unusual length allowed her to carry 50 percent more cargo than other boats while still maintaining the shallow draft necessary to clear the sandbars and riffs in the Yukon River. The original Klondike ran aground near Lake Laberge in 1936 and was destroyed.

The company immediately built a carbon copy, Klondike II, which operated from 1937 to 1952. She carried cargo and passengers from Whitehorse downstream to Dawson City, 460 miles, in a day and a half, making one or two stops for wood. On the return trip, the steamboat would proceed first to Stewart Landing, 70 miles past Dawson City, where she loaded sacks of silver-lead ore brought down the Stewart River from the Mayo Mining District. The upstream trip back to Whitehorse took four or five days and six wood stops. When an all-weather road was completed between Dawson and Whitehorse in 1950, trucks took over the transporting of the ore. The Klondike was extensively refurbished as a cruise ship, but the plan was 20 years too early to capitalize on the Yukon's burgeoning tourist trade. Now the Klondike II sits in permanent retirement on the banks of the Yukon River in Whitehorse. Parks Canada has carefully restored her and they now provide very interesting guided tours. At the end of the tour, I had to pass a quiz before the tour director would give me the "I toured the Klondike" certificate. So if you take the tour, pay close attention to the ship's cargo capacity (300 tons), dates (built 1936), engine horsepower (525 horsepower) and speed (10 knots).

CHAPTER 12

A 125-YEAR-OLD PARROT THAT SPOKE ITALIAN

A raging forest fire closed the Alaskan Highway and delayed my neighbor, Karla Reichert, and my cousin, Linda Chigi, who were riding the bus from Anchorage to Whitehorse. They finally pulled into Whitehorse Monday morning, 12 hours late. Karla, an occupational therapist working in the Dayton school system, had just completed the school year and she planned to cycle the last leg through Alaska with me. Linda, my cousin from Lockport, Illinois, always wanted to see Alaska and came up to help Connie support us in the van. After they put their bags in their room and freshened up, they joined Connie and me for some sightseeing. I took my fourth day off from riding in 40 days and we set out on a quick tour of Whitehorse before driving to Skagway, Alaska, 100 miles south on a sightseeing jaunt.

Linda loved the way Whitehorse was built along the river--the neat houses, clean streets and attractive shops. She even checked the local papers for job openings.

"I'd move here except I wouldn't like to deal with their money (Canadian)," Linda said. "It's all different colors!"

We followed the Klondike Highway (Route 2) south from Whitehorse. The miners dreamed of constructing a road over one of North America's most difficult mountain ranges after the 1896 discovery of gold in the Klondike. It took more than 80 years to complete the 110-mile scenic highway between

124

Skagway and Whitehorse. Engineers completed the first three miles of a rough road in 1914 after several aborted attempts. Gradually they built additional sections over the next 50 years. Finally, the U.S. and Canadian governments worked together to complete the last 50 miles of road by 1978. Crews had to blast parts out of the sheer mountainside. A tour-bus driver provided a colorful assessment of the road conditions: "Between Carcross and the Old Venus Mine is 11 miles of sheer terror, believe me!"

Emerald Lake, the most beautiful lake I've ever seen, is located about 40 miles south of Whitehorse. The lake bottom is covered with a white marl consisting of decomposed shells and clay. Reflection of the light from this white layer produces an array of blue and green colors that are so vivid they look artificial. Emerald Lake is not only world renowned for its unique beauty, but it must also be in the extra-terrestrial guide book. On July 2, 1998, three men were constructing a cabin overlooking the lake when one noticed an extremely bright reflective object flying around, perhaps 20 feet above the treetops. When he spotted the UFO, it swooped down the mountainside and zoomed a few feet over the workers' heads. In those few seconds all he could say was "look, look, look" and it was gone. The object was the size of a softball, highly reflective, almost blinding and appeared to have a metallic finish.

In Carcross, population 420, we stopped at the Cinnamon Cache for a snack. I bought a giant, fresh-baked cinnamon bun that was delicious. Their billboard featured a rear-view caricature of the husband-wife owners with the message, "Best Buns in the Yukon!" I agreed. As I ate my bun, I asked the owner about Carcross.

"It was originally called Caribou Crossing and the post office shortened the official name to Carcross. We had some small gold strikes in the area back in 1897 when the prospectors were headed for the Klondike and a number of them decided to stay," the owner explained.

"The next excitement occurred when they built the Alaskan Highway in 1942/43. Lots of men and machinery passed through here. Our most famous resident wasn't a prospector or miner, it was a parrot named Polly. Captain James Alexander carried the parrot over the Chilkoot Pass in 1898 on his way to the Klondike. In 1918, Alexander, who owned the Engineering Mines and was living in Carcross, asked the owners of the Caribou Hotel to take care of Polly while he and his wife made what was to be a short business trip to Juneau aboard the coastal steamer, Princess Sophia. The Princess Sophia sank near Juneau and all 463 people aboard perished. Polly lived out her life in Carcross at the Caribou Hotel. She became known for her hard drinking, ability to speak Italian, sing operatic arias and swear like a sailor. Eventually she quit talking to adults, except when someone asked if 'Polly wants a cracker?' she would scream 'Go to hell!' Otherwise she only talked to children. They say Polly was 125 years old when she died in 1972," the owner concluded.

A little beyond Carcross we entered the mountains and passed a number of very active and spectacular waterfalls sending a rainbow spray of mist across the road. There was still snow in the mountains, but it was melting fast. About 100 miles from Whitehorse, we passed the U.S./Canadian border and White Pass Summit, the highest point on the highway at 3,292 feet. Just past the summit, we stopped at Moore Creek Bridge, named for the founder of Skagway, Captain William Moore. The bridge is a cable-stayed design across the 110-foot canyon, high above the river. Support is provided entirely from the south bank of the gorge. It looked as if they forgot to build the other half of the bridge.

The town of Skagway, which derived its name from the Skagway River, was the gateway for the Klondike gold rush back in 1897. Today, the town has been renovated to maintain the look of an 1800s boomtown, but with the convenience of a 1990s tourist-shopping complex. Fire, the scourge of many

Half a bridge across Moore's Creek in the Yukon.

historic Alaskan towns, never ravaged downtown Skagway, leaving an authentic Gold Rush atmosphere. The old, false-front buildings now house a variety of tourist shops, restaurants, bars and sightseeing companies.

Skagway prides itself on being a place where "Gold in the Yukon!" still echoes from the steep canyon walls; where the sounds of the barroom pianos and boomtown crowds ring out in the night. Skagway is a place where the romance and excitement of yesteryear lingers around every street corner--around every bend in the trail (according to the tourist brochure).

Historic Skagway saw tens of thousands of fortune-seeking prospectors during the Klondike Gold Rush of 1897/8. Here, the stampeders piled off steamships, eager to head overland to the Yukon gold fields on the White Pass Trail. However, before the lonely men could leave town, they faced the temptations of 80 saloons, the lure of painted ladies, and the quick fingers of gamblers and thieves such as Soapy Smith and his ruthless gang.

We bought postcards and a few souvenirs before heading back to Whitehorse along the Chilkoot and White Pass Trails taken by the gold rush prospectors. It is a scenic ride today, but was a hellish trail in the winter of 1897 when the prospectors hiked it. Over 100,000 prospectors came to Skagway planning to strike it rich in the Klondike. Only about 40,000 of those prospectors ever made it to the Klondike to stake a claim and only approximately 100 of those actually struck it rich.

Why the Yukon? Prospectors had been searching the west for a new bonanza since the 1849 gold strike in California. They found gold in Oregon, Colorado, Montana and British Columbia. When those gold fields petered out, the next logical move was to follow the mountains north to Alaska and the Yukon. In the summer of 1896, Robert Henderson discovered a high concentration of gold on Gold Bottom Creek near the Klondike River. He alerted other miners as he went back to Joseph Ladue's trading post on Sixtymile River for supplies. One of the prospectors Henderson talked to was George Carmack. George and his three First Nation relatives, Dawson Charlie, Snookum Jim and Carmack's wife, Kate, set out for Gold Bottom. They stopped to check a small stream they crossed named Rabbit Creek and found a fair quantity of gold. George suggested that if Gold Bottom didn't pay off, they should return to Rabbit Creek. Staking a claim near Henderson's on Gold Bottom, they began working the gravel. The results were less promising than Rabbit Creek so they returned there. At Rabbit Creek they filled a shotgun case with gold in a short while. Carmack cut stakes and established his claim on August 17, 1896. Other prospectors in the area heard about Carmack's highly productive claim and soon hundreds of claims were staked near Carmack's. Because of the isolation of the Yukon, it was a year before the outside world knew of the gold strike. Only when Carmack and a few other prospectors arrived back in

Seattle with their pockets bulging with gold did the rest of the world succumb to gold-rush fever. Syndicates were formed to finance the trip for one member of a group to the Klondike to stake a claim.

The people who made money during the gold rush were the steamboat companies, suppliers and saloons along the way. While over two million ounces of gold were taken out of the Klondike area in 1898, most of that was recovered from a small number of very productive strikes. By 1899, the rush was over and miners headed for new gold strikes in Nome, Alaska, or back to the U.S. where the country was embroiled in the Spanish American War.

When one of the shopkeepers in Skagway learned that I was biking across the Yukon he proceeded to relate a tale he had heard about biking during the gold rush. "By late summer 1899," the shopkeeper began, "the Klondike gold rush was winding down. All the easy gold had been extracted, and it took companies with heavy equipment to wring the gold out of the less productive gravel. With the news of a new strike in Nome, Alaska, the miners rushed to catch the last paddlewheel steam boat down the Yukon River before the winter ice closed that highway to boat travel. After the freeze-up, the hardiest men set off to hike the 2,000 miles between Dawson City and Nome while the more resourceful rode dogsleds.

"One adventurous miner named Ed Jesson noticed a bicycle in the window of the hardware store in Dawson City and decided to buy it. He spent several days learning to ride the bicycle in Dawson and then set out on the iced-over Yukon River for the Bering Sea. The day he left, the temperature hung around minus 20F as he pedaled 50 miles. The roadhouses along the river were spaced at 25-mile intervals so Ed planned to eat lunch at the first roadhouse and stay overnight at the next each day. On his second day out, the temperature dropped to minus 50F and the grease in his bearings froze. Luckily, Jesson was rescued by a passing dogsled and hitched a ride to the Alaskan community of Eagle. He stayed in Eagle a few days until the temperature warmed up and then started biking down the river again.

"One day he encountered a tailwind and completed his 50 miles by noon. Another day while speeding along with a tail wind, he crashed into an ice ridge near the riverbank and broke his handlebars. Undeterred, Ed fashioned new handlebars from a spruce branch and continued on. At Kaltag, Alaska he left the river and headed across the frozen tundra for Nome. His pace slowed considerably on the rough tundra trail, but 30 days after he left Dawson City, Jesson arrived in Nome. There is no record of whether he struck it rich in Nome, but in any case Ed had a marvelous adventure to tell his grandchildren."

The Yukon prospectors were hardy souls who lived off the land. There were only a few trading posts or villages in the Yukon in the 1800s and fewer doctors or dentists. An aging Irish miner lost all his teeth during a bout with scurvy. One day he shot a bear near his cabin. The ingenious miner extracted the smaller teeth from the bear's skull and using the metal from a tin plate, fashioned a set of false teeth for himself. Then he proceeded to eat his winter supply of bear meat with the bear's own teeth.

Another of the colorful prospectors who participated in the Klondike Gold Rush was William C. Gates from Red Wing, Minnesota. Bill went to the Yukon in 1895. He happened to be washing dishes in a log hotel in Circle, Alaska, in 1896 when word of the gold strike arrived. The next morning he started poling a boat up the Yukon River toward the gold strike. Arriving at the strike area after the good claims had already been staked, he and six other men offered to buy claim number 13 (considered unlucky) on Eldorado Creek from another prospector for $40,000. The original claim holder accepted the offer. He and his partners soon paid off their debt from the diggings and each had $20,000 worth of gold in their pockets.

Bill hired other miners to work his claim on a percentage while he moved to town and flaunted his wealth.

After squandering away his fortune, Swiftwater Bill, a nickname he earned for his ability to handle a boat in rough water, headed for Alaska and found another incredibly rich claim. Again, he gave away and squandered his second fortune. Then he traveled to Peru where he prospected for gold and silver, making several very profitable strikes. In 1935, when in his sixties, Swiftwater Bill was murdered in Peru at the site of another of his rich strikes. Why didn't he settle down and enjoy the fruits of his labors? Many prospectors were really driven by the "search" for riches, not by the finding.

The two writers best known for their description of the Yukon and the Klondike gold rush are Jack London and Robert Service. Both spent time in the Yukon, experiencing its harsh winters and rugged beauty.

Jack London was born into a poor family in San Francisco in 1876. In his youth he ran two paper routes and did odd jobs to earn money. At 12 he learned to sail on San Francisco Bay and at age 16, lived the life of a young hooligan, drinking in the waterfront bars and sleeping with a mistress. He spent a year aboard a sealing boat, worked in a cannery and a jute mill and traveled to the East Coast and back as a hobo.

The thing that set Jack apart from the other wayward teenagers was his love of books and his desire to write. At age 17, he wrote an article about a typhoon he experienced aboard the sealing boat. The article won first prize in a writing contest and intensified his desire to learn. He went back to high school, but after one year decided he could learn more at the public library. By intensive study at home, he passed the entrance exam to the University of California. After a year in college, he dropped out of school. News of the Klondike gold rush had reached California, and Jack persuaded his sister, Eliza, to loan him enough money to buy a ticket to Skagway and the year's worth of supplies necessary to enter the Yukon. He carried his

131

2,000 pounds of supplies and equipment up the Chilkoot Pass, built a boat and floated down the chain of lakes to the Yukon River.

He spent the winter in a cabin on Split-Up Island at the mouth of the Stewart River. While he and his three partners tried to work gold claims, their main occupation was to stay alive through the bitter winter living on their meager supplies of beans, bacon and sourdough bread. Jack made an 80-mile trip to Dawson City to register their claim and stayed there for eight weeks. During that time, he became acquainted with sourdoughs, dancehall girls and millionaires who struck it rich. The stories he heard, along with his own keen observations, would be the basis of his future books. He returned to the cabin and helped work the claim through the winter. His only profit from this effort would be his memories of the frigid hikes over icy trails, life in a tiny cabin, dog teams passing through the settlement, cabin fever, death and acts of heroism. Those memories would help him produce one of the best collections of literature about the Klondike gold rush.

After a year in the Klondike, crippled with the effects of scurvy, Jack decided to head back to civilization. He floated down to Dawson City on a log raft and then built a small boat and sailed down the Yukon River to St. Michael where he caught a steamboat for California. Arriving home without gold, he started writing about the Klondike, the Yukon and the hardships that the miners endured. Within a few years he became the highest paid, best-known writer of his time. In the next few years he produced 50 volumes including *The Call of the Wild, White Fang, To the Man on the Trail and To Build a Fire.* Jack died of uremic poisoning in 1916 at the young age of 40. The final passage from his *The Call of the Wild* (London, 1988):

"When the long winter nights come on and the wolves follow their meat into the lower valleys, he may be seen running at the head of the pack through the pale moonlight of glimmering borealis, leaping gigantic above

his fellows, his great throat a-bellow as he sings a song of the younger world, which is the song of the pack."

Robert Service, the opposite of Jack London, was born into a well-to-do family, well-educated and lived the "good life." The one thing in common between the two men was their ability to tell a gripping tale about the harshness of the Yukon; London in prose; Service in verse. Service was born in Lancashire, England, in 1874, two years before London was born. Service worked at a bank in Scotland and immigrated to Canada in 1896. He bounced around Canada, the U.S and Mexico while the Klondike gold rush came and went. In 1904, he was working for a bank in British Columbia when they transferred him to Whitehorse, Yukon. Whereas London hiked, struggled and sailed to the Yukon in 1897, Service rode a comfortable steamship and train over the same route in 1904.

Over the next five years, he listened to tales of adventure and hardship. As he walked the gold rush trails around Whitehorse, he *"felt poetry all around him."* Soon after, he wrote *"The Shooting of Dan McGrew"* for a church concert. The church elders felt the poem was too rough to read in the church. Even the Whitehorse Star newspaper declined to publish the violent poem. Service continued to write other ballads about the desperate struggles of the Yukon, *The Cremation of Sam McGee, The Call of the Wild, The Spell of the Yukon, and The Parson's Son.* He sent his collections of poems to his father who had immigrated to Toronto and asked him to find a printing house to print a booklet of poems he could give to his friends in Whitehorse. The publisher had 1,700 orders for the booklet even before the printing was completed. Published in 1907, Service's poems were an instant success. Even before setting foot in the Klondike goldfields, Robert Service became the voice of the prospector. His poems rang with an authenticity of personal experience. He described the land, its inhabitants and how they felt in soul-catching verse. He created the mystique of the Yukon.

In 1908, the bank asked Service to take a position in Dawson City. Fast slipping into decline, Dawson City had dwindled from a peak of 30,000 residences in 1898 to fewer than 4,000 by 1908. In Dawson City, Service listened to grizzled veterans of the great gold rush reminiscing about the glory days of lonely men toiling underground and hiking to town with heavy pokes of gold. They looked back on their hardships and the whole panorama of the gold rush with an accuracy not possible while it was happening. The dancehall girls and miners reminisced while Service listened and recorded the details. His bank requested he return to Whitehorse in 1909 and take over a manager's position. Service had saved up $10,000 from his royalty fees and decided to leave the bank and spend his time writing. Even at this point, he had already become the best-paid poet of all time.

Robert Service wrote for four more years in Dawson City before leaving the Yukon for good. He continued to write poetry after that, moving to France and marrying. He died in 1958 at the age of 84. The poem I believe best describes the Yukon and the long winter nights is his *Cremation of Sam McGee* (Service, 1949).

There are strange things done in the midnight sun
By the men who moil for gold;
The Arctic trails have their secret tales
That would make your blood run cold;
The Northern Lights have seen queer sights
But the queerest they ever did see;
Was that night on the marge of Lake Lebarge
I cremated Sam McGee.

CHAPTER 13

WATCH OUT FOR THE BEARS

"Should we ride the mountain bikes today or the road bikes," Karla asked at breakfast.

"I prefer the mountain bikes because of the rough roads," I said.

"But we can make better time on the road bikes."

"The vibrations from the rough road shook me to pieces a week ago. The mountain bikes are better suited for these roads."

The mountain bikes won. Karla and I biked up Two-Mile Hill and out of Whitehorse on a cool, cloudy and calm day at 15-18 mph with a slight tail wind. It was nice to be riding with a partner again. Karla suggested we draft off each other to conserve energy so we rode in-line, close together and switched lead every four or five minutes. That worked great. We could rest while drafting and ride faster while leading, increasing our speed a couple of miles per hour.

Linda and Connie were waiting for us beside the highway near the village of Champagne. As we biked up, I saw Linda running around the parking lot swinging a yellow, plastic badminton racket.

"What in the world are you doing?" I asked.

Zap, phitt, crackle, zap!

"I'm killing mosquitoes," Linda said with a grin of satisfaction on her face.

135

Karla's first day of biking in the Yukon was a chilly one.

Karla had brought along the mosquito zapper she bought in the Virgin Islands. It was a battery operated contraption that looked like a small tennis racket with wire strings. By pressing the button on the handle, the operator charged up the horizontal and vertical strings. When the charged strings came in contact with a mosquito, it fried the bug with a loud ZAP, just like the blue-light electric bug zapper that hangs on your back porch. It looked ridiculous for Linda to chase mosquitoes with a tennis racket, but it was super effective. She could completely clear an area of aggressive, blood-sucking mosquitoes in a few minutes.

Connie served us juice, fruit and snack crackers, and filled the water bottles on our bikes while Linda waged war on the mosquitoes.

From the tourist information book we learned that Indians have occupied the Dezadeash River Valley around Champagne for at least 5,000 years. They called it Shadhala ra, which meant "Sunshine Mountain Camp."

Approaching Haines Junction, we discovered mile after mile of wild flowers along the edge of the highway. Brilliant reddish-purple sweet peas, blue lupines and yellow dandelions covered mile-long patches of the roadside. The warm weather brought them into bloom. We had encountered a few flowers before, but this day there were millions. We arrived at Mountain View Inn early in the afternoon after a great 98-mile ride. This was Karla's first day of riding in the Yukon and she did a great job. She is a stronger biker than I am and drafting behind her made my day easier.

Nestled at the base of St. Elias Mountains, Haines Junction currently has a population of 800 full-time residents. The town, situated at the junction of the Haines and Alaskan Highways, came into existence in 1942 to support the building of the Alaskan Highway. Today, Haines Junction is the headquarters of Kluane National Park and the staging point for wilderness recreational activities including river rafting, canoeing, glacier tours, horseback rides, hunting and fishing.

Whoever designed the Mountain View Motel placed all of the windows facing the dusty road to the south. They should have looked west toward the beautiful range of snow-capped mountain. As it was, we had to walk outside our room to get the beautiful mountain view.

At supper we asked about the status of the forest fire at Burwash Landing that had delayed Linda and Karla's bus.

"The road was closed for a couple of days, but they are letting traffic through now," the waitress said. "You may have an hour's delay, but you can get through."

On a brilliant, cool Wednesday morning we rode out of Haines Junction at 15 mph. About five miles out of town the road started uphill to a 3,200-foot high summit. The hill didn't seem very steep, but it just kept going up and up and up. As we gained altitude, our speed slowed from 15 mph to 12, to 10 and finally 8 mph. A line of snow-capped mountains stretched along on our left for the entire day. Brown snowshoe rabbits appeared

137

at 100-yard intervals along the road (they turn white in the winter). They sat by the side of the road as still as statues with their big ears twitching back and forth like radar antennas. When I approached within 20 or 30 feet of them, they would dart across the road and disappear into the woods.

Karla and I finally crested the summit after two hours of exhaustive pedaling and stopped for a rest and snack. Refreshed, we coasted down and down and down to the shores of Kluane Lake, Canada's largest. Biking beside Kluane Lake we could see Mount Logan in the distance, Canada's highest peak at 19,550 feet. The mountain valleys that feed Kluane Lake contain numerous glacier ice fields, some 60-miles long.

"Watch out! There's a bear and her cub ahead," a biker riding the other direction warned us, as we rode along Kluane Lake. Sure enough, a mile ahead we saw two brown lumps of fur eating grass alongside the road. The 500-pound mama grizzly bear looked up as I biked past her, 15 feet away. I held my camera to the side and snapped a picture of her as I whizzed by. I didn't think it prudent to stop and ask her to pose. She decided to cross the road just as Karla biked past. I was afraid Karla would get between the mama and her cub, but the bear sauntered peacefully across the road 20 feet behind Karla and looked for something to eat on that side. We stopped down the road where Connie and Linda had parked and took more pictures with a telephoto lens. A car drove up with a large German-Shepherd dog hanging out the car window. As it stopped, the dog jumped out of the window and started running toward the bears, barking. They ambled off into the woods as the driver called her dog back to the car. I was surprised the lady didn't realize how dangerous it was to allow her dog to chase the bears. A camper was killed by a grizzly just the week before in this area. Grizzlies are dangerous, especially when they have a cub.

A little further up the road, Connie and Linda watched a lynx lope majestically across the road and down to the lakeshore. The snowshoe rabbit population is very high this year. They are

We passed a mama grisly and cub 15-feet off the highway.

the lynx's favorite fast food and there were more of them in the area than normal this year.

A bus passed us and honked a friendly greeting.

"That's Henry!" Karla shouted as she waved to the bus. "He drove us from Anchorage to Whitehorse last Sunday. He said he'd be heading back to Anchorage today."

Biking along the lakeshore, we caught the strong smell of wood smoke. Ahead we saw a thick layer of smoke hanging over the lake like a low rain cloud. The smoke was from the big forest fire that started Saturday around Burwash Landing---over 50 miles away, the one that delayed Karla and Linda's bus. The Royal Canadian Mounted Police closed the road from Beaver Creek to Destruction Bay so firefighters could battle the blaze.

Riding beside the lake, we crossed mile-wide glacier riverbeds with thick layers of ice still clinging to the banks of the narrow, active river channels.

139

Ten miles from the forest fire the smoke became very thick.

As the smoke became thicker, Karla and I put on smoke masks, the white filter-paper type people use when painting. They did a good job of cutting down the amount of smoke we inhaled. We probably looked funny to the people passing in cars, but it made breathing much easier.

The authorities still had a roadblock set up about eight miles outside of Burwash Landing. The village, which had a population of 100 people before the forest fire, came into existence in 1904 when gold was discovered on nearby Fourth of July Creek. This lakeside community became a supply and accommodations center during the building of the Alaskan Highway. Now, the smoke was so bad they were escorting cars through in one-way convoys with a pilot truck in front and in back of the pack. Karla and I loaded our bikes in the pilot truck and rode with the driver, Bruce.

A blaze flared up like a kerosene torch as we passed.

"Normally I do highway maintenance around Whitehorse," Bruce told us, "but they've called in about 100 people to fight this fire."

"How big an area is burned?" I asked.

"About a ten-mile by ten-mile area with Burwash Landing at the center."

"How did the fire start?"

"It started in the dump at Burwash. Someone was burning trash and it got out of hand."

When we passed through Burwash Landing, I saw four or five houses burned to the ground, several vehicles destroyed and telephone poles burned in two. The fire burned trees on both sides of the road, but occasionally it left small pockets of trees untouched on each side. When I rolled down the window to take a photo, the heavy smoke burned my eyes and made it difficult to breathe. We passed many small blazes still burning in the

141

woods. At the western edge of the fire zone, a new blaze started in a stand of spruce trees as we drove by. The flames leaped 200 feet in the air as the trees flared up like kerosene torches. We could hear it crackling and feel the heat of the blaze 500 feet away. A spotter helicopter flew overhead and radioed for a fire crew to fight the blaze.

The Burwash Landing Lodge where we planned to stay had burned down. We were lucky to find rooms at the Kluane Wilderness Village 25 miles further up the road. Before supper we walked to Scully's Burl workshop, known as the burl capital of the Yukon. Burls are the bulbous growths on limbs of spruce or pine trees. Hundreds of tree trunks with unusual burls lined the fence outside the small workshop. Scully, a 75-year-old Yukon artist and humorist, fashioned imaginary animals from the burl-encrusted trunks and limbs as he has for the past 20 years. He also publishes books of humorous sayings he has collected over the years, such as: "Some people stay longer in an hour than others do in a week."

Scully was sitting on the front porch of his shop carving a burl as I walked up. We talked about the Yukon, Kluane Lake and burls for a while.

"We saw a wolf running along the woods by the road today," I said. "Do you have any problems with them around here?"

"No, not really," Scully replied. "Though I did have a little problem with them last winter. I took my boat up Kluane River to hunt for moose. When I saw moose tracks along the shore, I beached my boat and followed the fresh tracks up the mountain. It was late in the day when I finally caught up with a huge bull moose. He had a rack on him that was enormous. I snuck up close and dropped him with one shot. By the time I gutted him it was getting dark and starting to snow. I knew if I left him until the next day, the wolves would get him so I decided to spend the night there. The temperature dropped and an icy wind came up. I wasn't prepared to sleep out in those

142

Scully told me the wolf story while he carved a burl.

sub-zero temperatures so I decided I'd climb inside the moose's belly to survive.

"Well, I fell asleep and was having a pleasant dream when I woke up with a start! There was a terrible ruckus outside. I peered out of the belly-slit and there was a whole pack of wolves snarling, snapping and tugging on the moose. The first thing I knew, I could feel the moose moving. Those wolves had the moose on the drag!

"From inside the moose's belly, I caught hold of the tailbone with one hand and his Adam's apple with the other and realized I could steer the thing, like using the rudder on my boat.

"With the wolves dragging it at a full gallop, I steered that dead moose right down to my boat. Then I jumped out and shot the leader before he could get me. The other wolves scattered in all directions.

143

"I put the moose and the wolf in my boat and floated down river to the road where I parked my truck. The wolf hide and moose rack are hanging on the wall in my shop, if you'd like to see them," Scully concluded with a smile. I went into his shop. Sure enough, there hung a big moose head and a wolf pelt.

Karla, Linda, Connie and I ate a delicious supper with the conversation revolving around the forest fire. None of us had been that close to a big fire before. I went to bed early and was dreaming peacefully when...

"Boom, boom, boom, boom!"

The curtains flew open from the blast and sunlight flooded my darkened room. I woke wide-eyed from a deep sleep, jumped out of bed and swung the door open. A dozen half-dressed motel guests peered out their doors as a big cloud of brown dust rose about a mile away.

"Looks like they're blasting at the rock quarry," one of the locals said. I thought we were being bombed or hit by lightning. The blast rattled the entire building.

It rained hard during the night. The road was still wet as Karla and I started biking on a cloudy, cool and windy Thursday morning. We crossed the Donjek River, a wide, silty, rapid glacier runoff stream. The 2,000-foot thick, mountaintop glaciers from the Wisconsin glacier period, 10,000 years ago, are slowly melting. There was construction on the other side of the bridge, ten miles of gravel road with big rocks. We stopped for a photo alongside one of the giant Caterpillar trucks with tires twice as tall as I am. They haul 75 tons of rock in a single load. The construction crew let Karla and I bike through the area. About 20 miles up the road, we came to another construction area. A young flag lady named Jodi stopped us and said it would be 20 minutes before we could go through.

"The pilot truck just left to escort the northbound cars through," she said.

"What's your dog's name," I asked, pointing to a little white poodle wrapping his leash around her legs.

144

The truck had tires 10-feet high and carried 75 tons of rocks.

"It's Fritz," Jodi said. "He belongs to the grader driver. I watch him while the guy works."

We talked to Jodi until the pilot truck came back with a bunch of southbound cars. Karla and I loaded our bikes in the back of the truck; I rode in the truck with Ralph from Whitehorse while Karla rode in the van with Connie and Linda. Ralph said they could only work on the road 100 days a year because of the long, cold winters. The crews work ten hours per day, seven days per week for four weeks and then get a week off.

"What's the best paying job on construction?" I asked.

"Driving the road grader. It pays $21 an hour."

"That's not much to live on when you have to survive a 250-day long winter," I replied.

"I help my buddy cut wood in the winter and live on my unemployment check," Ralph responded.

"I noticed you use different size rocks for fill on the highway. Where does the fill come from?" I asked.

"We usually blast it out of the mountain right along the edge of the highway. The blaster is told how big the rocks are supposed to be and he drills the slab to get the right size rubble. We use the really big rock, the size of a truck, for the deep fill. Then we cover that with basketball-size rocks. The top layer is golf-ball size crushed rock."

I thanked Ralph as he handed down our bikes.

Just north of the White River Bridge we came upon a cable-car system snaking over the mountain. The big buckets were used to move copper and silver ore from a mine beyond the mountain to huge storage silos near the highway. I've seen cable cars like these moving mountains of ore near Death Valley. There was no way to tell how long the cable cars had been silent, but the system still looked in good shape, as though it could start operation tomorrow if needed.

Three trumpeter swans and a beaver swam in a lake while two coyotes sneaked along the edge of the road by Snag Junction. Snag Junction was named when the government surveyors had trouble getting through the dense undergrowth to survey the area 100 years ago. In 1942, the government built an airfield in Snag as part of the Northwest Staging Route. The airport was abandoned several years ago. The other distinction of Snag is that on February 3, 1947, the temperature dropped to minus 81F, the coldest ever recorded in North America. Locals reported that the freezing of human breath produced a continuous hissing sound and that as people moved around they left a vapor trail of breath 100 to 500 yards long lasting three of four minutes. One fellow threw a bowl of hot water in the air and watched it fall to the ground as tiny, round ice pellets. Rubber became as hard as concrete. If you tried to twist the dog's leather harness, it would snap instead of bending.

"I remember this restaurant very well," Karla said as we stopped for lunch at the 1202 Motel in Beaver Creek. "We sat

On day 45 we crossed from the Yukon into Alaska.

here eight hours on Sunday night while the highway was closed."

Beaver Creek is Canada's westernmost community and the gateway to Alaska. The current population of 125 people are employed in running the tourist accommodations, mining and supporting the 24-hour-a-day Canadian Customs and Immigration border activity.

After lunch, Karla and I biked another 20 miles to the Yukon/Alaskan border. We labored through several stretches of rough gravel road along the way. At the Alaska border, we stopped for a photo of the "Welcome to Alaska" sign. Back in the good, old U. S. A. Connie and Linda met us at the border and drove us back to our motel in Beaver Creek, Yukon, where we celebrated the completion of the Canadian portion of the trip with a steak dinner and apple pie ala mode.

147

CHAPTER 14

HOW DID CHICKEN GET ITS NAME?

The time changed from Yukon Daylight to Alaskan Daylight when we biked across the Alaskan border. We gained another hour. I love these 25-hour days, especially when they include 23 hours of daylight! A light drizzle fell as we pedaled along on a cool, cloudy and calm Friday morning. Small spruce, pine, poplar and birch trees covered the rolling, hilly terrain.

The early morning sun peaked out from the clouds. For the first time, I realized we were so near the Arctic Circle that the sun was coming up almost directly in the north, just 25 degrees off of true north. We rode passed a juvenile moose eating its breakfast beside the road. It looked up unconcerned, and then went on eating the tender shoots at the water's edge.

The road became significantly smoother on the Alaskan side of the border. Time to switch bikes. We flagged down Connie and Linda when they drove by in the van and switched from the mountain bikes to the skinny-tired road bikes. These bikes allowed us to ride 3 to 5 mph faster than the mountain bikes, as long as the road wasn't bumpy. Karla was particularly happy to be back on a high-performance road bike. Her chronic knee problem flared up again and the larger-frame road bike put less stress on it. We pedaled past several huge, desolate burned areas from the 1990 Tok forest fire. Wood crews cut the damaged trees to salvage the usable lumber.

One of the 40 moose we met along the Alaskan Highway.

At Tetlin Junction we stopped for a snack where the Top of the World Highway from Dawson City, Yukon, connects back up with the Alaskan Highway.

"Did you come down by way of Chicken?" the lady in the gas station asked as I paid for our snacks.

"No, we came the southern route through Beaver Creek," I replied. "How did the town ever get a name like Chicken?"

"Well, the way I heard it, the locals originally called the town Ptarmigan, pronounced 'Tarmigan' after the grouse-like bird that's common to these parts. When the settlement got its first post office and it was time to record the official town name, nobody could figure out how to spell ptarmigan. They were pretty sure it didn't start with the letter "*t*," but they didn't have a clue about the spelling. The miners jokingly referred to

149

ptarmigan as chicken when they served it for dinner so someone suggested they call the town Chicken. The idea was unanimously adopted and the town was officially named Chicken."

"How big is Chicken?" I asked.

"Used to be a thriving mining town, but there are only about a dozen residences and one saloon now. Mostly, tourists stop there on the way to Dawson City."

The road from Tetlin Junction into Tok was flat and smooth. Karla led and I drafted off her as we raced into town at 20 mph. We were flying.

"What does Tok mean?" I asked Sugar, the desk clerk at Young's Motel.

"The story is that when Lt Allen was surveying Alaska for the U.S. Army back in 1885, he came to a creek and asked his Indian guide, 'What is this?' The guide, who knew just enough English to think the question was foolish, answered 'Tokai' the native word for creek. Lt Allen dutifully marked Tok Creek on his map. When the town sprung up in 1942 while they were building the Alaskan Highway, it took its name from the creek."

"What is Tok known for?" I asked.

"It's called the 'Gateway to Alaska'," Sugar continued. "There are only two roads between Canada and Alaska and they both pass through Tok. We are also the dogsledding capital of the world. We do more breeding, training and mushing than anywhere."

To celebrate our arrival into Alaska, we ate supper at Fast Eddie's where I ordered Alaskan king crab legs and a T-bone steak. Bike riding gave me a big appetite. Fast Eddie's started as a pizza parlor, but now is a huge, first-class, full-service restaurant. After supper I returned to my room to write in my journal. There was a knock at the door. A distinguished-looking couple introduced themselves as Joan and Albert Reyerse from nearby Gakona.

"We met your cousin, Jeanne Weber (Linda's mother), in Hawaii 18 years ago," Albert said with a noticeable foreign accent. "Jeanne phoned us and suggested we visit with you and Linda when you came through."

"Well, I'm glad you came by," I said. I called Linda and the four of us reminisced about Hawaii and travel. The Reyerses own Bon Voyage Travel Agency in Alaska.

"I can't place your accent," I told Albert. "Where were you born?"

"I was born in Indonesia with Dutch parents," Albert explained. "I grew up in Holland and immigrated to America."

"How is the travel business?" I asked.

"It's getting to be very cut-throat," Joan replied. "With everyone on the Internet, people can book their own trips cheaper than we can. Most of our clients now are older couples who want us to plan an extended foreign trip for them. We are only operating the agency part time and will probably retire from it soon."

Saturday had all the makings of a tough day: a 111-mile segment, a 4,000-foot high mountain and a strong head wind. The day started pleasantly enough, cool, partly cloudy, calm and flat for the first 12 miles. Then, the wind picked up as we reached the 2,000-feet altitude level. By the time we reached 3,000-feet, we were only riding 10 mph. After cresting at 4,000 feet, the head wind held us to 13 mph even while riding downhill.

Dozens of ravens sat in the trees and stood beside the road, dining on the unfortunate snowshoe hares or squirrels that were squashed on the highway. The ravens are much larger than our crows, about the size of a chicken, and very bold. They hopped only a few feet off the road when I biked up and hopped right back to their meal as soon as I passed. An article in the Guide to the Goldfields (Vergara, 1999) states that ravens are considered the most intelligent, most widely distributed and most adaptable birds in the world. They are found from the Arctic

Circle to the mountains of Central America. The ravens in the Arctic have developed horny insulated soles on their feet that are six times thicker than tropical ravens so they can endure the sub-zero temperatures.

These birds can survive in an urban environment as well as in the wilderness. They are monogamous, live for up to 40 years and are very choosy about their potential mate. The female is completely dependent on the male to feed her and her young for about a month each year.

One example of how clever the ravens are involves the climbers on Mount McKinley. Ravens have learned to recognize the special kind of bamboo markers that mountaineers use to mark food caches in the snow. After finding a marker, the raven will dig down through three feet of snow to raid the cache. When the bird sees a native hunter in the woods, it will often fly ahead to spot game and give a loud call to attract the hunter, knowing that it will get a share of the kill that is left behind. Ravens will work together to harass wolves who have killed an animal. As the wolves try to chase off the most aggressive ravens, the others will sneak in and steal from the carcass.

Ravens have a larger vocabulary of calls than any other bird or animal except man. They use a specific yell to call a juvenile, a quork to advertise territorial limits, a rack to warn their young to hide and a soft whining call in intimacy between birds friendly with one another. Their loudest call is "soups on" to attract others when they locate food. I never tire of watching and listening to them.

At one rest stop I talked to some locals who warned us to be on the lookout for bears.

"A biker was riding along a wilderness trail near here last week," the fellow said. "He came around a curve and ran directly into a bear. The guy rode his bike off the trail right into the river to get away from it. He lost his bike, but saved his skin. Be sure to give any bears you meet a wide berth."

152

Our support team brought the tire pump, food and water.

I ran over a sharp rock halfway to Delta Junction and my rear tire went flat. To reduce the weight on my bike, I stored the tire pump in the van. Karla had to ride ahead, find the van and have Connie come back with the pump to where I was disabled. When I changed the tube, I also put a new tire on my rear wheel. The previous 3,000 miles of hard riding had worn the tread completely smooth and the tire was paper-thin.

We completed our ride along the Alaskan Highway at Delta Junction, mile-marker 1423, at 4:00 p.m. Our motel wasn't at the intersection so Karla stopped in a laundromat to ask directions. Women think it is okay to ask directions--men just keep riding around hoping to stumble on their destination. Actually, a scientific study published in a Neuroscience Journal found that men use a different part of their brain than women do to navigate. Men visualize a map and use geometry to get where they are going; "the ballpark should be north-west of here." Women tend to navigate by landmarks; "turn right at the drug store then left at the grocery."

"Four miles up the road," a patron told her.

What's another four miles after a 107-mile ride? At Delta Junction, the Alaskan Highway connected to the already existing Richardson Highway from Valdez to Fairbanks. We biked up the Richardson Highway to the Alaska 7 Motel completing a tough 111-mile ride. The addition of 22 sections of gravel road and one flat tire resulted in a 12-hour day that left Karla and me exhausted.

Delta Junction developed from the construction camp established there during the building of the Alaskan Highway. There was already a small settlement in the area called Buffalo Center because the U.S. government had released 28 buffalo there during the 1920s hoping to create a free-ranging Alaskan buffalo herd. The experiment succeeded. Today, there are 400 buffalo roaming the surrounding countryside.

For supper we drove to the Buffalo Restaurant; I ordered a buffalo steak. It was as tender as beef and a bit leaner. We celebrated another milestone on the bike trip: into Alaska and off the old Alaskan Highway.

On Father's Day, we started up the Richardson Highway to Fairbanks at 4:30 a.m. My daughter-in law, Connie, gave me a Father's Day card before breakfast. Later in the day, my daughter and wife called with best wishes. I hadn't seen my family for a month and a half and the Father's Day greetings boosted my morale.

We biked past Rika's Roadhouse on the Tanana River at Big Delta shortly after we were underway. It is one of only two remaining roadhouses on the old Valdez-to-Fairbanks trail. During the gold rush days there were 30 roadhouses along that trail. John Hajdukovich built the original roadhouse at Big Delta

154

back in 1904. Shortly after it opened, a Swedish immigrant named Rika Wallen came to work there. In 1923, she bought the roadhouse for $10 plus several years back wages John owed her. Rika operated the roadhouse until the 1950s when she retired. She continued to live there until her death in 1969. Now the roadhouse and Wallen's homestead are part of a museum in the State Park at the site.

It started raining mid-morning. The first few big drops of rain falling on the warm pavement smelled so good. I don't know if it is ozone or dust that causes the smell, but it brought back very pleasant memories.

We saw six moose during this day's ride, including a bull moose who almost ran me down. Karla was in the lead; I rode about 100 yards behind as we started down a long, steep hill. The moose came out of the woods just after Karla passed and attempted to cross the road. Since my bike blocked his way, he turned and trotted alongside me, down the hill for a minute or two. He apparently decided I wasn't a threat and turned to cross the road. As he started across in front of me, I screamed and slammed on my brakes. His back leg just grazed my front tire as his 1,000-pound frame lumbered across the road. I was still shaking when I caught up with Karla at the bottom of the hill. It would be difficult to explain the moose tracks across my back at the emergency ward.

Business must be bad along the Richardson Highway. The only thing selling was "For Sale" signs. Every lodge, roadhouse, gas station and general store we passed was closed and had For-Sale signs out front. The village of Richardson was totally closed. We also noticed that the rest stops along the Richardson Highway had no toilets or trash bins, whereas the rest stops in the Yukon were very nicely equipped.

Around noon we biked past Eielson Air Force Base, 30 miles from Fairbanks. A dozen F-15 fighters and A-10 ground-support aircraft were parked on the ramp. While I worked for the Air Force, we flew our C-135 military plane to Eielson each

155

year to test new aircraft radios in the cold temperatures. It took 7 hours to fly from Dayton to Eielson AFB compared to the 396 hours it took me to bike the same distance.

A stop at the North Pole, a small community between Eielson AFB and Fairbanks, was mandatory. The village was named North Pole by a clever developer hoping to entice manufacturers to set up factories there so they could advertise that their products were built at the North Pole. So far, no major manufacturer has opened a factory, but the year-round Santa House does a brisk business in Christmas items. Karla, Connie, Linda and I all bought postcards and Christmas ornaments during our stopover. North Pole was also the location of the radio station where I passed my message to the Carlsons.

Traffic was horrible for the last 15 miles into Fairbanks-- 600 cars/hour whizzed past us at 60 mph. I just held my breath and stayed far over on the shoulder of the road. At 1:30 p.m., we arrived at the Bridgewater Hotel--93 miles in 9 hours. A great day of biking!

I ordered prime rib for my Father's Day supper at Captain Bartlett's restaurant. The aged beef almost melted in my mouth. We celebrated with good food, excellent service, pleasant company and a relaxed atmosphere.

The Fairbanks Visitor's Guide explains that back in 1901, while Italian prospector Felix Pedro was digging for gold he saw the smoke from a steamboat on the distant Chena River and headed down the valley in hopes of buying supplies. Meanwhile E.T. Barnette was arguing with the riverboat captain because the captain claimed the river was too shallow to go any further. The captain dumped Barnette and his supplies on the shore. Pedro found Barnette and told him there were many other prospectors in the area. Barnette set up his trading post on the banks of the Chena. Soon after that, Pedro struck a rich claim and a full-fledged stampede was underway.

Barnette's trading post grew into a town and within five years was the biggest and busiest one in Alaska. In an effort to

156

score some political points with Alaskan Judge Wickersham, Barnette convinced the town folk to name the town Fairbanks in honor of Wickersham's friend, Charles Warren Fairbanks, who was an U.S. Senator from Indiana and later Vice President. Today, Fairbanks has a population of 33,000 and a bustling economy based on mining, tourism, the oil pipeline, education (University of Alaska) and the military (Fort Wainwright and Eielson AFB).

A day off! What's that? Monday was only the fifth day in my 51-day trek that I didn't bike--a rare luxury. Karla and I reorganized the van for the final three-day push to the Arctic Circle---minimum clothes, bike parts and food for the finish. Connie went off to visit her cousin, Debbie, who came to Alaska in the military and ended up staying in Fairbanks after her military commitment was over. I searched the yellow pages and located a freight company that promised to ship my bikes back to Dayton after I finished the ride. It was hard falling asleep Monday night. I kept thinking up questions to ask the Carlsons about their 23 children when I met them the next day.

CHAPTER 15

RAISING 23 CHILDREN IN A LOG CABIN

Raising 23 children in a log cabin with no electricity, running water or indoor toilets, now that's a story worth telling! It started when, by chance, I met a lady in Galena, Illinois.

"You could stay with the Carlsons north of Fairbanks," Diane Dahlby told me. "They always have room for one more. Joe and Nancy don't have a phone so you'll have to call the radio station in North Pole and put a message on 'Trapline Chatter.' They'll get back to you."

I called the radio station and left a message saying I'd like to stay overnight with the Carlsons on June 22. A week later, I called the radio station back and learned that the Carlsons had agreed to my visit. Biking up the Elliott Highway from Fairbanks, I saw the sign to Joy and pulled into the gravel driveway. Karla, my support driver, was waiting for me in the van. We walked into the Wildwood General Store and asked where we could find the Carlson's Cozy Cabins?

"Just follow the driveway down about 100 yards and you'll find my folk's cabin. I'm Cherie Carlson Curtis and this is my daughter Carrie."

"Hi. I'm Allen and this is Karla."

"Oh, you're the biker," Cherie said.

"Yeah, I'm the one."

Karla and I walked down the gravel lane through a stand of black spruce trees to a rustic log cabin and met Joe and Nancy Carlson.

158

"Please come in and sit down. This is Molly who is five; Angela, seven; and Simon, ten," Nancy said as the three children hid shyly behind her.

We sat in their comfortable living room that was dominated by a big wood stove and shelves overflowing with school texts and general-interest books. The log walls were covered with pictures of their 23 children and numerous grandchildren.

"So how did this all happen?" I asked.

"Well," Nancy began, "I always wanted a big family. As a child I decided I wanted to be a missionary and run an orphanage. One of the books I read was titled, *The Family Nobody Wanted*, by a minister's wife who adopted 12 children of different races. My heart went out to kids who didn't have the kind of family that I had been blessed with.[1]

"Right after we were married, Joe joined the Navy. During the next three years, his assignments took us to California, Florida, Midway Island and Japan. We were blessed with two homegrown children during this time, Andy and Cherie, and adopted a seven-day-old baby in Japan. Assigned back to California, we adopted hyperactive, nine-year-old Greg and his four-year-old sister Julie. Joe decided to get out of the Navy at that time so the seven of us moved back to Minnesota to be near our parents and live on a farm. Our family was adjusting to farm life with our five children when a call came from California--'Did we want to adopt Greg's other brother and sister?' Sure! So Katy and Brad joined our family.

---

[1] Karla and I talked to Joe and Nancy Carlson and their children for several hours. The basic story they told us is recounted here. I used information from Nancy's book "Joy Abounds" and Cherie's book "Homestead Kid" to fill in a lot of the details I forgot or didn't ask during our visit.

Joe and Nancy Carlson with 12 of their 23 children.

"Life progressed okay on the farm, but the children seemed to have trouble in school. There were daily calls from the principal about troubles the boys were getting into. They were good at home, but couldn't seem to get along with the other children at school. Joe and I talked about home schooling. Home schooling wasn't allowed in Minnesota in 1973 so we decided to move to Alaska where it was allowed.

"Joe bought a 1951 GMC school bus and converted it into a travel trailer. We loaded the bus with our seven children, all our household goods, 18 dogs, 20 goats and headed up the Alaskan Highway for Fairbanks. Our first winter was spent in a one-bedroom cabin near Fairbanks with no electricity, running water or indoor toilet. Joe said the kids might as well get used to roughing it because we planned to build a similar cabin of our own in the woods.

"Joe found a job as a welder in Fairbanks that paid good wages, but everything was so expensive in Alaska we were barely scrapping by. I was pregnant again and decided to try a home delivery since Joe had no hospital insurance and there wasn't money to pay the doctor. Just in case there were any complications, we decided to drive the bus to the hospital parking lot and Joe delivered baby Zack there. We walked into the hospital with the baby to get a birth certificate.

'How old is the baby?' the records-clerk asked as she nonchalantly typed up the form.

'Oh, about 30 minutes,' Joe replied.

"She jumped up and shoved a chair under me and frantically called the doctor.

'I'd like to examine you,' the doctor said.

"I told him we didn't have insurance or enough money to pay him.

'There won't be any charge,' the doctor assured us.

"He examined me and said everything was okay. He gave us a good scolding and made me promise we'd have a doctor for the next delivery before he let us go.

"A few days after Zack was born, we packed all our possessions back into our bus and drove up the Elliot Highway to the 40-acre plot we bought here in Joy. There, we started building the cabin you're sitting in now. Joe, my dad and the older boys used chain saws and axes to clear the land and cut trees for the cabin. The women used hatchets and handsaws to trim the limbs from the logs and cut the underbrush. It was a crash course on wilderness living--hauling water in five-gallon jugs from the spring, living without electricity and building an outdoor john. I learned how to preserve food by canning 30 salmon and a whole moose that fall. With Joe still working in Fairbanks, it took us four months to complete the 24-foot by 24-foot cabin. While that sounds small for two adults and eight children, it was spacious compared to the bus or the one-bedroom cabin we were renting," Nancy said.

"What do you do for a refrigerator or freezer?" I asked.

"We built a spud locker," Joe replied. "It's a small, insulated building covered with sod. With the permafrost underneath, it stays 40 degrees year-round. All our vegetables, potatoes, milk and perishables are stored in there. Our freezer consists of lowering a 55-gallon barrel down a hole in the permafrost. Of course, during the winter the back porch serves as our freezer."

"How did you do the home schooling?" Karla asked.

"The education department from the State of Alaska provided us the books and supplies," Nancy explained. "There were four boxes for each child and one for me, the teacher--41 boxes in all. There was a lot of one-on-one reading and instruction required so it became necessary for the older children to help each other, while Joe and I worked with the younger ones. They studied four or five hours a day all 12 months of the year to cover all the required subjects. I had to give them tests and send the results to the education department. It was a lot of work, but I think the children received a good education. Several have gone on to complete college and all of them are working at good jobs."

"I understand a lot of the children you adopted were hard to place cases," I said.

"Yes, most of them were abused, had physical or mental problems or had been adopted before and returned to the agency as unmanageable," Nancy said. "Our approach was to give each child definite responsibilities. Abused children don't know much about caring or loving because they haven't been nurtured or cared for themselves. We raised goats, pigs, ducks, geese, dogs, cats, horses, and each child had to care for some of the animals. In addition to the animals, each child had kitchen duties, house-cleaning duties and worked a shift at our general store. For the first time these children felt wanted and needed. If they didn't water, feed and change the bedding their animals would suffer or die. Having another living thing depend on you is powerful therapy for a troubled child. Besides their chores, our children took advantage of the unique opportunities of living in the wilderness. Zack and Nathan built a dogsled team with money they earned on their trap line. They use the sled to run the trap line. We agreed to provide feed for the dogs if they would haul all our firewood in on the dogsled.

"Jade, a 13-year-old orphan from India, came to us after being placed twice and returned as too disruptive. Within a year she adjusted to our way of life and started studying extra hard so she could complete two grades a year and catch up to the grade she should have been in at that age. It was very enlightening to see America through Jade's eyes.

"We adopted Galia from a Bulgarian orphanage at age 16. She had been in the orphanage since age three. The Bulgarian orphanage didn't have enough food or clothing for all their orphans so the children had to fight to get something to eat or wear. Galia had fought for her very survival for 13 years and it was a big adjustment to move into our house with all our other children and accept the idea that she could get the food she needed without grabbing or fighting for it. With the help and love from all of us and the animals, she gradually adjusted."

"How many children do you have at home now?" I asked.

"Just the three you met earlier," Joe replied, "Molly, Angela and Simon. We were surprised to get them because they are Native American and usually the tribe doesn't want native children raised by a non-native family, but, these children had physical problems. The tribe agreed that we could adopt them. They brought our family to 23 children and I'm not sure we're done yet," Nancy said with a smile.

"You have a most unusual and amazing family," I said.

"What a privilege and awesome responsibility it is to raise our children during a time when kids are regarded as a liability, rather than the precious God-given treasure they are," Nancy replied.

Nancy led us to her kitchen and started preparing supper on her huge, wood-fired cook-stove. Institutional-size pots and

I fell in love with 5-year-old Molly Carlson.

pans hung from the log beams and hundreds of mason jars of preserved vegetables, fruits and meats lined the walls. The smell of the wood fire and stew cooking on the stove made me realize how hungry I was.

After supper the children took Karla and me on a tour of the outbuildings and the farm. Simon showed us his favorite tree where he built a tree house. Angela took us in the chicken house and collected eggs from the nests of the squawking hens. I had forgotten the unique smell of a hen house, not bad, just like chickens. Molly showed us through the barn where the Himalayan cats, Shelties, Bichons, Labs and other dogs lived. Along the way we visited the Russian boars, geese and goats. Then the children took us up the drive to where the famous old school bus that the family drove to Alaska was parked in the woods. It hasn't run for 20 years, but they still use it as a storage shed and play house.

After the tour, Molly put her tiny hand in mine. It fit perfectly! She led me to the one-room log cabin where I would spend the night. Then she picked up a broom and swept it out while I unpacked and made the bed. When she left, I realized I had fallen in love with that beautiful, industrious child and the whole Carlson family.

CHAPTER 16

TEN MILES OF THE ALASKA PIPELINE ARE MISSING

An 800-mile-long steel snake, the Trans-Alaska Oil Pipeline, materialized just outside Fairbanks at a tourist display with photos and an explanation of the construction. For the next three days, the ever-present pipeline led me through the black spruce forest toward the Arctic Circle.

Geologists had been looking for oil in Northern Alaska since the 1920s, (Ewing, 1996). In 1968, an Atlantic Richfield (ARCO) and Humble Oil (now Exxon) exploration team discovered oil on state land on the North Slope near Prudhoe Bay. One geologist said the natural gas escaping from the well sounded like four jets flying overhead, (Cole, 1997). A confirmation well drilled seven miles away tapped into the same massive oil formation and established the enormous dimensions of the strike. It turned out to be the largest oil find ever in North America and the eighteenth largest in the world.

The fact that the oil lay in one of the most remote spots in the world provided a first-class challenge to the oil companies. The technology to extract the oil from the North Slope of Alaska and get it to market did not exist in 1968. There were no roads across the tundra and beneath was permafrost, soil that was permanently frozen. Normal steel piling would crumple like soda straws when driven into the frozen ground.

166

I stopped to inspect the oil pipeline just outside of Fairbanks.

Options for getting the oil to market included a proposal from General Dynamics to build a fleet of nuclear-powered submarine tankers to run under the ice and ideas from Boeing to build immense 12-engine jet tankers to fly it out. An ice-breaking tanker, the S.S. Manhattan, made an experimental voyage around the Northwest Passage to see if direct shipment was feasible. It was not.

The oil companies opted for a more conventional solution, a pipeline from Prudhoe Bay to an ice-free port at Valdez, Alaska. The Trans-Alaska Pipeline System (TAPS) was formed by ARCO, Humble and British Petroleum (BP) in 1969 to design and build the 800-mile pipeline. They immediately ordered $100 million worth of 48-inch diameter pipe from Japan, one of the few bargains in the entire project. TAPS was expected to cost $900 million and take three years to build, with completion scheduled for 1972. Before the end of 1969, Amerada Hess, Home Pipeline Company, Mobile Pipeline

The pipeline snakes along beside the gravel support road.

Company, Phillips Petroleum and Union Oil joined the original three companies to share the pipeline.

TAPS filed for federal right-of-way permits in 1969, but early in 1970 several environmental and Native Rights groups filed lawsuits to stop the construction. Congress approved the Alaska Native Land Claims Settlement Act in 1971 to settle the Native Rights claims. Environmental arguments continued until 1973, when Congress intervened and voted to limit further court delays. President Nixon signed the Trans-Alaska Pipeline Authorization Act in the fall of 1973 just as the OPEC oil embargo created gas shortages in the U.S. Gas prices shot up 40 percent, and many Americans were shocked to learn that we were so dependent on imported Arab oil.

In the spring of 1974 (if you call 40 degrees below zero *spring* in Alaska), construction of the haul road between Prudhoe Bay and the Yukon River began. By the summer of 1974 trucks could drive the narrow, gravel Elliott Highway from Fairbanks to Livengood, the Dalton Highway to the Yukon River and the Haul Road all the way to Prudhoe Bay. Truckers earned $10,000 a month hauling 80-foot long sections of 48-inch pipe north.

As soon as the pipe arrived and the support camps were completed, welders from Oklahoma, Arkansas and Texas began welding the half-inch thick pipe together. Welding pipeline is an art learned after a long apprenticeship. There are pipeliner's unions such as Local 798 from Tulsa, Oklahoma that provide welders for pipeline construction around the world. The 798ers made $18.75 an hour straight time in Alaska, far above the hourly rates for other unions on the pipeline and several times the going wage in the lower 48 states in 1975. "I thought about becoming a brain surgeon," a 25-year-old pipeliner from Bald Knob, Arkansas said, "but it wouldn't pay me enough." Members of the 798 used to boast that they could weld anything from a broken heart to the crack of dawn!

While the welders and truck drivers made exceptional wages, even laborers, cooks and bus drivers got rich working at the construction camps. They were paid top wages, provided a free room, served excellent meals and received premium pay for overtime. A former $10,000-a-year school teacher could save $15,000 to $20,000 a year working on the pipeline. The workforce peaked at about 28,000 people in 1975 with a total of 70,000 people employed during the entire construction project.

As with all big projects completed in a hurry, there was considerable waste on the pipeline. Welders complained they sat around for hours waiting for pipe to be delivered, for welds to be inspected or for decisions to be made. Scheduling work along the 800-mile pipeline was a major task complicated by poor roads, limited communications facilities and bad weather. There were stories of faulty welds, but in fact, very few of the over 100,000 individual welds developed leaks. The facts didn't stop Johnny Carson from reporting on his "Tonight Show" in 1976 that the pipeline construction boss had recently ordered a 700-

mile long roll of duct tape from a Thrifty Drug Store. There was also the ever-present theft problem that plagues all big projects. In addition to tools, supplies, food and clothing, occasionally a company truck would turn up missing. Comedian Mark Russell reported that "Ten miles of the Alaska pipeline are missing. Authorities are determined to find it, even if they have to search every pawnshop in the state. The foreman on the job posted a sign on the bulletin board that said, 'To whoever took the ten miles of pipeline, put it back where you found it and no questions will be asked'."

I stopped and inspected sections of the pipeline alongside the road and was amazed at the unique support structure. Since the ground is permanently frozen in most of Alaska, heat from the pipeline would melt the permafrost and the pipeline would sink in the resulting quagmire. To prevent the thawing, the pipeline is insulated, jacketed and installed on Vertical Support Members (VSMs). The VSMs contain two-inch diameter heat pipes filled with anhydrous ammonia to transfer the heat from the oil to the air. The pipes are fitted with aluminum radiators to improve the heat transfer. The 78,000 VSMs do the job and keep the permafrost frozen.

Construction of the Alaska Pipeline was a monumental engineering task often compared to the challenge of building the Panama Canal or the Great Wall of China. When the American Society of Civil Engineers compiled the "Seven Civil Engineering Wonders of the United States" in 1994, the pipeline made the list. The nation's longest pipeline crosses three mountain ranges, 34 rivers and 800 streams. It bisects Alaska from Prudhoe Bay to Valdez carrying 10 percent of the oil used every day in the United States.

The pipeline statistics are amazing: (Alyeska, 1997)
Oil discovered at Prudhoe Bay: March 13, 1968
First pipe laid: March 27, 1975
First oil flowed: June 20, 1977
Cost: $8 billion

Time to complete: 3 years, 2 months
Earth moved: 93 million cubic yards (equivalent to the
    Suez Canal)
Truckloads of pipe: 19,000
River crossings: 34 major, 800 minor
Length: 800.3 miles
Depth to Prudhoe Bay oil formation: 9,000 feet
Pipeline capacity: 9 million barrels of oil
Speed of oil flow: 5 mph
Flow rate: 1.4 million barrels per day
Travel time: 6.2 days
Materials shipped to Alaska: 3 million tons
Gravel used: 73 million cubic yards
Total workforce: 70,000
Permits required: 832 state, 515 federal
Special animal crossings: 554
Buried pipeline: 380 miles
Earthquake resistance: to 8.5 Richter Scale
Pumping stations: 11
Maximum operating pressure: 1,180 psi
Oil temperature: 116 degrees F
Tankers loaded: 50 per month
Time to load tanker: 18 hours
Oil loaded to date: over 13 billion barrels
Oil value: $260 billion at $20/barrel
Percent of domestic oil production: 20 percent
Percent Prudhoe Bay oil taken from ground to date:
    about 50 percent.

171

CHAPTER 17

CROSSING THE BLUE-DASHED ARCTIC CIRCLE LINE

A cold drizzle pelted my face and shocked me awake as I pedaled out of town and up the Steele Highway in the dim dawn at 4:00 a.m. Tuesday morning. Karla drove the support van while Connie and Linda stayed behind in Fairbanks visiting relatives. The highway started as a four-lane paved road with a huge hill right on the edge of town. That set the mood for the next three days--the hills never quit. The two-lane Elliott Highway separated from the Steele Highway in the village of Fox and deteriorated to gravel 30 miles later.

It was sobering to read the sign on the combination gas station/restaurant/convenience store outside of Fox, "LAST GAS TO THE ARCTIC CIRCLE." I stopped for a cup of hot tea and bought some morale-building snacks.

Most signs of civilization disappeared 30 miles north of Fairbanks. Farms, houses and electric wires gave way to trees, streams and wildflowers. I rode up two- and three-mile-long hills all day in low gear at 4 or 5 mph. Coming down the gravel hills at 20 mph was very bumpy, but didn't take long.

A huge beaver swam back and forth across a placid stream, posing for pictures as I biked up the road. Cars and trucks zoomed by kicking up clouds of dust and spraying me with gravel. I pulled over to the side of the road and ducked my head as they passed. A lady in a truck coming the other way stopped to warn me about a moose and calf on the road ahead.

172

"She'll chase you if you get near her calf," the lady said.

I kept watching ahead and finally spied the mother and baby placidly munching grass beside the road. The mama moose walked unconcerned into the woods as I biked up and the calf trotted obediently behind her.

I stopped for a snack at the trailhead of White Mountain Trail, 40 miles north of Fairbanks. That trail is designated for hiking, skiing and dogsledding--NO motorized vehicles. At mile 55, I passed the old gold-mining camp of Livengood. In its heyday, Livengood consisted of a dozen log cabins and one saloon run by a fellow named Sam. In addition to sandwiches and a good selection of booze, the saloon boasted the only house of prostitution north of Fairbanks.

"Sam had a ham and cheese sandwich on his menu for $3.50 and a cheese and ham sandwich for $4.00," Diane Dahlby told me. "One day I asked Sam what the difference was?

'Fifty cents,' Sam said."

After the gold panned out and Sam died, Livengood became a ghost town. The state bought the property in the 1980s and turned the camp into a transportation center for their road maintenance trucks. They tore down all the cabins and the saloon and donated the logs to homesteaders.

Just past Livengood, the Dalton Highway joins the Elliott Highway. Fifty miles straight ahead, the Elliott Highway dead-ends into Manley Hot Springs--population 50. I took a right turn onto the Dalton Highway toward the Arctic Circle and Prudhoe Bay. While I waited at the end of the day for Karla to pick me up, black clouds of mosquitoes swarmed out of the swamps and descended on me. I swatted them for several minutes until Karla rescued me and drove me back to Joy. We stayed up late Tuesday night talking to Joe and Nancy Carlson about their homestead and adventures. It was still light when I set my alarm for 4:00 a.m. and fell asleep.

Wednesday morning I overslept for the first time on the entire nine-week trip. My alarm clock stopped during the night and I didn't wake up until after 5:00 a.m. Karla and I ate cereal for breakfast and then she drove me up to the Dalton Highway. As I started biking the rough, gravel road I passed a road sign: Yukon River 56, Coldfoot 175, and Deadhorse 414. The Arctic Circle didn't even make the sign. The hills were even steeper than the previous day, requiring me to shift down to my lowest gear, 1-1, several times. I pedaled up the hills at 4 mph gasping for breath and my legs complained about the workout. The early-morning sun shown through the fog covering the roadside swamps and gave off an eerie, golden glow. As the occasional truck whizzed by, I ducked my head so the rocks thrown by its tires bounced off my biking helmet. Clouds of dust obliterated the road for a minute or two. A water-spray tanker drove by mid-morning and wet the road, cutting down on the dust for the next few hours.

I stopped for a snack at a wide spot in the road where a couple named Jim and Donna had parked their camper. As we chatted, they told me they lived in Ohio until they recently retired to Arizona. They were on their way to see the Arctic Circle just like me. A few miles up the road a man standing alongside a blue pickup truck flagged me down.

"Hi. Are you the guy biking up from Ohio?" he asked.

"Yeah, I started from Dayton."

"We saw the article in the Cleveland paper back when you started," his wife said. "I cut it out and told my husband we'd look for you as we drove up. We drove by you a few miles back and I asked my husband to stop and wait here. Oh, I'm so glad we finally found you. I think your ride is exciting."

"I've always wanted to see the Alaskan Highway and this trip is a dream come true," I told them. "How was your drove up from Ohio?"

"It's the prettiest trip we've ever taken," she replied.

At least two dozen snowshoe hares hopped across the road as I biked along and a few long-bodied weasels shot across like spring-loaded slinky toys.

174

The gigantic Yukon River, Alaska's longest, appeared as I topped a hill at mile marker 56. The river has a milky appearance as a result of the silt pouring in from the glacier rivers. As the glacier slides along, it grinds the rock into a fine powder and the melt-water carries the rock powder down the glacier rivers. Early-day riverboat captains complained that the glacier river water was too dry to drink and too wet to plow.

Archaeological evidence indicates that people have been living along the Yukon River for the past 20,000 years. The river and many settlements in the area take their name from the Athabascan Indians and Inupiat Eskimos who first peopled the riverbanks. Numerous native and gold-mining settlements are still only accessible by air or river travel.

I threw a bottle with a note in the Yukon River at Whitehorse ten days before and stopped on the bridge to see if it had made the 1,000-mile trip yet. No bottle. The river appeared wider than the Mississippi and requires a 2,295-foot long bridge to span it. A work crew was laying a new wooden deck to replace the old, rotted floorboards.

The remains of Five-Mile Camp, one of the oil pipeline camps used during construction, appeared five miles north of the river. Bulldozers and dozens of gravel trucks were swarming around the old camp, building a modern tourist campground. The nearby pipeline airfield lies right next to the road and is still usable. A yellow sign and light warns motorist to "STOP and hold for air traffic when light is flashing." No aircraft this morning.

As I crossed the dozens of streams flowing through the swamp-laced land, I stopped to enjoy the perfect reflection from the mirror-like surface of the placid water. The reflected colors of the trees, mountains and sky appeared more vivid than the real-life scene. Hundreds of bank swallows swooped back and forth under the bridge feasting on the clouds of mosquitoes.

About 15 miles beyond the Yukon River, I spied Karla and the van parked in a gravel turnoff. The Arctic Circle lay just

40 miles and five hours ahead and I considered riding on to finish the trip a day early, especially with 24 hours of daylight. However, my leg muscles informed me that it would not be wise to ride any more today. I pulled into the turnoff and loaded my bike in the van. Karla drove back to the Yukon River where she reserved the last room available at the Yukon Ventures Motel. The small, simply furnished room was part of the pipeline camp barracks back in the 1970s. The pipeline company agreed to remove all buildings from the oil camps when they finished construction. These barracks came from Five-Mile Camp.

For supper we drove back to Five-Mile Camp and sampled the cuisine at the Hot Spot. Teressa and Julie come up from Fairbanks every summer to operate the eatery and gift shop out of two trailers.

"We make more money here than working in Fairbanks and it's nice living in the wilderness for the summer," Julie said.

They served us a platter-sized hamburger (Alaskan size), potato chips, pickles and a Pepsi. Dessert consisted of homemade cheesecake and pie.

Sleep eluded me Wednesday night, as I kept thinking about getting to the Arctic Circle the next day. Would I be disappointed? Would it be what I expected? Was I ready to finish this adventure? The fact that it was light all night, and that people were wandering around outside working on their trucks and cars didn't help matters. I finally drifted off to a fitful sleep.

POW! The sound of a high-powered gunshot brought me straight out of bed. Looking out the window, I saw a middle-aged man with a scruffy beard walking by my window carrying a rifle. I have no idea who or what he was shooting at 1:30 a.m. The gunshot woke the dogs and now three of four of them started competing to see who could bark the loudest and longest. I stuck my head under the covers to escape from the mosquitoes buzzing around the room, the barking dogs and the daylight. At 3:00 a.m. I got up, dressed and ate breakfast.

176

Karla drove me to the point where I quit the night before and at 4:00 a.m., I was biking along the Dalton Highway toward the Arctic Circle. After 50 days of biking, I was really psyched up. I pedaled as hard as I could, made only short water stops and avoided eating any snacks to eliminate problems with my nervous stomach. As I headed up Finger Mountain, the hills became steeper. The mosquitoes swarmed around my head and legs when I slowed to 4 mph going up the big hills. They couldn't catch me when I rode along the flat or downhill.

A huge owl flew across the road in front of me and a red fox peered out from the edge of the woods as I biked by. Biking north, the terrain changed from a black spruce forest to treeless tundra. The Arctic tundra felt spongy when I stepped on it.

Halfway to the Arctic Circle, I stopped at a granite outcrop called Finger Rock. Finger Rock is one of hundreds of tors scattered across Alaska's interior. A tor forms as an underground granite mass. Due to earth movements, the granite fractures into huge blocks that are eventually exposed by weathering and erosion. Finger Rock is a 50-foot-high formation that looks like a hand with the index finger pointing south. The formation "points" in the direction of Fairbanks so early bush pilots like Wiley Post used it as a landmark, and it is even printed on the aeronautical charts.

About 9 o'clock I biked up what seemed like an endless hill at mile marker 111. I thought that was the last hill before the Arctic Circle, but no, there was a long downhill and another big hill at mile marker 114. As I crested the hill, I saw the sign announcing that the Circle was one mile further up a side road. With the sun shining brightly, I biked the last mile and triumphantly rode across the blue-dashed Arctic Circle line at 9:32 a.m. Alaskan Daylight Time, completing the 4,081-mile ride in 51 days. Karla documented the finish with a date-stamped photograph. The beautiful Arctic Circle sign shows a North-Pole view of the earth with the dotted Arctic Circle extending through Alaska, Siberia, Russia, Finland and Norway. The Arctic Circle,

At 9:30 24 June 1999 Allen crossed the blue dashed line.

at 66 degrees and 33 minutes north, is the point where the sun is visible for 24 hours only on the summer solstice, June 21st. North of the circle, it is visible for a longer period each summer. South of there, the sun is never visible 24 hours a day. Signs around the observation platform at the Arctic Circle described the four seasons in the Arctic and how the flora and fauna adapt.

I sat down in the sun, and with a warm glow of satisfaction, savored the finish and reflected back on the trip. My average mileage for the 46 days I rode was 90 miles a day. My longest distance was 125 miles in 10 hours and longest day was 14 hours of pedaling to ride 85 miles against a constant head wind. The prettiest part of the trip was the Yukon wilderness and the most interesting part was listening to the stories of the people I met.

CHAPTER 18

YOU'RE NOT GOING TO BIKE BACK TO OHIO?

I was euphoric! My year of preparation and 51 days of biking were over and I really made it to the Arctic Circle. I wandered around in a bit of a daze trying to convince myself I'd reached my destination. A few other tourists arrived at the circle. We chatted with a young man who just graduated from the University of Alaska at Fairbanks, a lady from Minneapolis who brought her cat named Bailey to see the Circle and a couple from Arizona. A tour bus arrived and we watched the look of amazement on people's faces as they climbed out of the bus and saw the bright blue dashed line running along the Arctic Circle.

Linda, Connie and her cousin, Debbie, from Fairbanks, promised to drive up and be at the circle for the finish. They hadn't arrived yet so we waited. In the mean time, Karla and I ate our picnic lunch of turkey baloney, potato chips and Pepsi. After lunch it became apparent some problem had befallen our crew so we packed up and headed back to town. We stopped at Joy where Joe Carlson presented us with a signed certificate verifying we made it to the Arctic Circle. I held Molly one more time and tried to convince Joe and Nancy to let me keep her. No luck.

We arrived back at Fairbanks late afternoon and found our support team waiting in our hotel room.

"What happened to you guys?" I asked.

Joe Carlson presented us with an Arctic Circle certificate.

"We started out at 5:00 a.m. to be sure we got there before you did," Connie said. "A little past Livengood, the truck hit a chuck-hole in the gravel road and broke the shock absorber on the front right wheel. It made an awful clanging and scraping noise as we tried to drive slowly on. I tried to flag down a truck or someone to take us up to the Arctic Circle, but no one stopped. Finally, we turned around and limped home at 15 miles an hour. We just got here an hour ago."

"We bought balloons, a ribbon for the finish line, champaign and cake to celebrate at the Arctic Circle," Debbie said. "Since we didn't make it we decided to celebrate here." A multicolor "Congratulations" sign stretched across the room, balloons hung from the ceiling and a huge bouquet of flowers decorated the table.

"Well, let the party begin!"

I popped the cork on the champagne and cut the cake. Two of Karla's friends, Angie and Vince, who are assigned to Eielson AFB, joined us as we ate, drank, chatted and celebrated. Great party!

When we ran out of champagne, I suggested Captain Bartlett's for supper. The prime rib and baked potato filled in nicely around the champagne and cake. As we sat and talked, I felt a warm glow all through my body. I'm sure it was the glow of satisfaction, not the champagne. It was still light when our party wrapped up (on June 24th it's light all night in Fairbanks). I went to bed and slept like a baby!

On Friday morning, I packed some of my bike accessories in a box Linda purchased from the post office and the staff at All Weather Sports packed my four bicycles for shipment. I delivered all five boxes to the shipping clerk at Omni Freight to ship back to Dayton.

"You're not going to ride them back to Ohio?" she joked.

In late June, sunset occurs at midnight in Fairbanks.

"No, one way was enough. How will the bikes go?"

"We'll truck them to Anchorage today. Tomorrow they'll be on a barge for Seattle. They'll truck them from Seattle to Dayton. You should have them in about two weeks."

Friday afternoon, Jamie Izak from Channel 11 TV in Fairbanks came over and filmed an interview about the bike ride.

We ate supper with my cousin, Jerry Revels, and his wife, Val. Jerry has lived in Alaska for the past 25 years, working for the John Deere equipment dealer. He told stories of miners buying front-loaders, bulldozers and backhoes.

"They pulled out a bag of gold dust and plopped it down on the desk as payment for the equipment." Jerry said. "We had to take the gold to the bank and have it assayed to figure out how much it was worth."

After supper we drove back to the hotel room and watched my biking interview on the 6 o'clock news (which wasn't shown until 8:30 p.m. because the baseball game ran late).

Early Saturday morning I walked down to the lobby to organize my trip notes while the others slept. An elderly gentleman named Clarence, who was waiting for a tour bus to take him to the Arctic Circle, introduced himself.

"I saw you on TV last night," Clarence said. "How far did you ride your bike?"

"Four-thousand miles from Ohio to here," I replied.

"This is the fellow we saw on TV last night," Clarence said to several others in his group. His friends asked questions, took my business cards and autographs. I felt a little embarrassed by all the attention.

At noon we drove 56 miles northeast from Fairbanks up a dead-end road to Chena Hot Springs. Alaska, the most geologically active state in the Union, boasts many mineral hot springs. Chena is one of three near Fairbanks (Manley Hot Springs and Circle Hot Springs are the other two). The Indians knew about the hot springs for thousands of years, but Chena was "discovered" by a geological survey team in 1904. With the gold rush in full swing in Fairbanks, crippled prospectors were looking for a place to soak away their arthritic aches and pains. A trail was cut to Chena and by 1911, the trip could be made from Fairbanks by dogsled in about 20 hours. The trail was improved and a regular stage run began with a round trip every ten days. The original resort consisted of 12 cabins, a bathhouse and stable. The mineral content of the 156-degree water is very similar to the famous Carlsbad springs in Bohemia. Now, the resort features rooms for over 100 guests, camping facilities, indoor and outdoor pools, a dining room, bar, gift shop and its own landing strip for light aircraft. Chena offers cross-country skiing, horseback riding, four-wheelers, mountain bicycles and hiking.

My priority was a hot mineral bath to soothe away some of my accumulated pains. Separate pools offered water

We panned for gold at Chena Hot Springs. Eureka!

temperatures from 85 degrees to about 112 degrees. I started low and worked my way up to the hotter water, as I became accustomed to the heat. It felt great to soak in the pools until I was as limp as a wet noodle.

"Let's go gold panning!" Connie suggested. That sounded like fun so we walked to one of the concession cabins operated by a bearded, grisly ex-miner named Ralph. He took us out to a water trough by the creek and dumped a small bag of gravel into our gold pans.

"You swirl the water around and shake the pan gently so the lighter sand and gravel washes out," Ralph demonstrated with his gold pan. "The gold is heavier and it'll settle to the bottom."

I started swirling and swirling and swirling. It took 15 minutes of hard work to reduce the pile of gravel in my pan to a

184

little bit of sand and a little bit of "color". In the bottom of my pan were 25 or 30 flakes of 24-carat gold. I was rich! Ralph carefully poured my precious gold into a small glass vile and filled the vile with clear water. The water tended to magnify my puny gold dust and make it look like it was worth the $10 I paid to pan.

After two days of heavenly relaxation, I recuperated enough to continue our adventure. The four of us drove back through Fairbanks and down to Healy, Alaska, near the entrance to Denali Park (Denali is an Indian word meaning "the high one"). We stayed at the Denali North Star, a set of huge dormitory buildings interconnected with covered walkways. The dormitory was originally located in the Bering Sea near Prudhoe Bay at the oil drilling camp. When the pipeline was completed, the oil company dismantled these perfectly good buildings and moved them to Healy.

We took the Denali Park shuttle bus tour of the park. Private cars are only allowed along the first 15 miles of the 90-mile long limited access park road so we parked our van at the visitor's center. The 6-million-acre park, larger than the state of Massachusetts, is truly impressive. When I first toured Denali back in the 1980s, I planned to "drive up Mount McKinley." I didn't succeed. To get an idea of how big and remote Denali is, there are no roads within 50 miles of McKinley's peak. Because of the cloud cover, many people spend a week in Denali and never see it. We were lucky on this trip--the clouds parted mid-afternoon and we caught a glimpse of the lofty peak. Another advantage of taking the bus, there are 20 pairs of eyes looking for the elusive wildlife. We spotted 10 caribou, 2 grizzly bears, 61 Dall sheep, a golden eagle, a northern harrier and 2 deer falcons. One of the caribou came running down a ravine toward the bus and galloped across the road right behind us. I guess he was late for lunch.

The next morning Karla and I decided to climb Mount Healy while Connie and Linda rested and shopped. About half

185

Two adult caribou playing bookends in Denali Park.

way up the rocky trail, we encountered three oriental girls running down the trail.

"Bear!" one of the girls shouted as she shot past us.

We continued cautiously up the hill. About two-thirds of the way up to the top, my sore muscles convinced me to turn around. Karla continued to the top of Mount Healy.

"The view was magnificent," she reported.

That afternoon we drove south along the George Parks Highway to Talkeetna, an Indian word meaning "river of plenty." The one-of-a-kind town of Talkeetna, population 300, is the major starting point for climbers tackling Mount McKinley. Hundreds of years ago, the Tanaina Indians established a village at the junction of the Talkeetna and Susitna Rivers. When the Alaskan railroad was built from Anchorage to Fairbanks in 1919, Talkeetna became a major railroad camp. Today, the town maintains its wilderness flavor with dozens of

A good view of Mount McKinley from Talkeetna.

real (1930 vintage) log cabins (half of the 26 downtown buildings are on the National Register of Historic Places).

Talkeetna became the natural starting point when climbing Mount McKinley became a popular sport in the 1950s. Since there are no roads up to the mountain, the logical access is by air. Talkeetna's 5,000-foot long runway is relatively close to the glacier where most of the mountaineers start their climb. During the summer climbing season, potential climbers are flown up to a glacier camp at the 6,000-foot level on the south side of the mountain. They set up camp and start moving their supplies up the mountain. Typically a climber will move supplies a few thousand feet higher each day and return to his lower altitude camp for the night. This allows them to acclimate to the altitude. Altitude sickness is a very serious problem that leads to headaches, vomiting, weakness and insomnia. While the temperature in Talkeetna may be 90 degrees during the summer, the upper slopes of Mount McKinley are perpetually snow-covered. Even in summer, the temperatures at the higher altitude drop below zero and wind-chill of minus 50 degrees is common. Approximately 1,000 climbers challenge the mountain each summer. About 50 percent make it to the 20,320-foot high peak. The mountain is very unforgiving--91 people have died attempting to climb it. Thirty-five of those have never been recovered. Amazingly, three Russian climbers made a successful winter ascent in 1998.

We left Talkeetna for Anchorage on Wednesday. Approaching Palmer, we noticed a tourist sign in Wasilla pointing toward the Iditarod Headquarters.

"Let's stop," Karla suggested.

We toured the Iditarod museum and from their video learned the background of that grueling dogsled race.

In January 1925, Dr. Curtis Welch diagnosed a diphtheria outbreak in Nome, Alaska and sent an urgent telegram requesting the antitoxin serum. Doctors located a large quantity of the serum in Anchorage. The only two aircraft located anywhere in Alaska had been dismantled for the winter so the Governor called the largest organization in the Yukon River area, the Northern Commercial Company, and asked them to organize teams of dogsleds to carry the serum to Nome. The train from Anchorage carried the serum to Nenana, near Fairbanks. Twenty different dog teams operated in a non-stop relay to carry the lifesaving medicine down the frozen Tanana and Yukon Rivers and then across the barren snowfields to Nome, 675 miles in five days. One musher, Leonard Seppala, and his dog team headed out from Nome to meet the team coming from Nanana, picked up the serum, turned around and headed back for Nome. When he finally handed the serum over to another team, Seppala and his dogs had traveled 260 miles without a rest stop. The serum arrived in Nome in time to save the lives of countless Nome children who had been exposed to the dreaded disease.

Joe Reddington organized the Iditarod Trail Sled Dog Race in 1973 from Anchorage to Nome to commemorate the 1925 serum run. Joe went on to win the Iditarod several times and at age 71 still finished in the top five racers. He has been driving dogsleds since he first came to Alaska in 1948. With his dogsled, Joe hauled freight, salvaged downed airplanes a piece at a time and hauled passengers. When someone bet him a dogsled couldn't make it up Mount McKinley, Joe mushed his team to the summit.

Joe Redington, the father of the Iditarod, died on June 24th, 1999, the day I crossed the Arctic Circle. We watched a TV special about Joe while resting at Chena Hot Springs. While at the headquarters we enjoyed a dogsled (wheeled) ride pulled by four Alaskan huskies and driven by Joe Redington's son, Raymie.

We also stopped at the Eagle River Tour Center for a nature walk. It is a beautiful park with gigantic cow parsnip flowers.

That afternoon we drove into Anchorage and realized we were in a big city again--heavy traffic and lots of activities. We walked down to the oceanfront and found Anchorage has a huge tidal flow similar to Maine. Several good-sized fishing boats sat in the mud several hundred yards from the water's edge.

On Thursday we took the train to Whittier for a glacier cruise. The Alaskan Railroad is a profitable state-owned corporation hauling passengers and freight over its 470-mile route from Seward to Fairbanks. The railroad was started in 1903 to haul coal and ore from the newly-discovered mines. The early railroad venture faltered and was purchased in 1915 by the Alaskan Railroad Company. That year, the tent construction site on Cook's inlet became Anchorage, which today holds half of Alaska's 600,000 population. They completed the railroad to Fairbanks in 1923 and upgraded it extensively during WW-II when the military moved to Alaska to protect it against Japanese attack. The military built a 12-mile spur from Portage to

Whittier on Prince William Sound to provide a second year-round ice-free port. Our train followed that spur through a two-mile-long tunnel to Whittier to catch our glacier tour. The comfortable train was full of tourists who were glued to the windows watching eagles soar along the picturesque Alaskan coastline on the right side and Dall sheep clinging to rugged mountain slopes on the left.

At Whittier, Linda, Connie and I boarded the Klondike Express catamaran while Karla waited for the Inland Marine Ferry to Glacier Island. The cat sailed out of Whittier and into Prince William Sound at a speed of 37 knots--very fast for a cruise ship. More time at the glaciers, less time enroute is their motto. The catamaran was perfectly stable; they guarantee no seasickness aboard.

"What's that in the water?" Connie yelled, pointing to several brown blobs near the ship.

"Sea otters," I said. "They're floating on their backs and have their pups on their chests."

We saw hundreds of cuddly sea otters throughout the day. Thirty minutes out of Whittier, we cruised up to the first of the 26 glaciers we would see on the trip. A mile-wide river of ice, 300-feet high flowed down the mountain and into the ocean. As we crowded the railing to get a closer look a **BOOM** rang out as loud as an artillery shot and a huge chunk of ice calved off the face of the glacier and splashed into the ocean. Everybody cheered.

"How old are the glaciers?" someone asked.

"The ice that just broke off is probably 100,000 years old," a crewmember explained. "Glaciers hold 75 percent of the earth's freshwater. In the United States, glaciers cover about 27,000 square miles of land mass, most of it here in Alaska."

"Are these the largest glaciers in Alaska?" another person asked.

"No, the largest glacier in Alaska, and for that matter in the world, is about 200 miles down the Alaskan coast. The

190

A huge chunk of the glacier calved of with a shot-like boom.

Malasina Glacier covers almost 3,000 square miles, larger than the entire country of Switzerland."

"How fast do these glaciers move?" was the next question.

"Most of these glaciers move a few inches a day. There are fast moving glaciers in Greenland and other places that move hundreds of feet per day."

"How thick are they?"

"Up in the Chugach Mountains where these glaciers form, they are probably a few thousand feet thick. The glaciers in Greenland and the Antarctic are several miles thick."

"Are the glaciers growing or shrinking?"

"For about the last 30 years, the climate in Alaska has been getting warmer and the glaciers are shrinking. Alaska has over 1,000 glaciers and only a handful have been carefully measured, but it does appear most are shrinking."

"What happens if they all melt?"

"Well, you'd be able to buy some beach-front property in Pennsylvania. The oceans would raise a couple of hundred feet if all the glaciers melted, but that's not likely to happen in the next few hundred years."

We ate a tasty buffet of chicken Kiev with all the trimmings while the boat motored to another glacier. As we approached the next glacier, the captain announced that whales had been spotted on the starboard side (that's right side for us landlubbers). Everyone rushed outside and to the right side of the ship. Four or five fins appeared as the killer whales breached the water and dove back under. The captain followed the whales into a bay. We watched them swim around for ten minutes before continuing on to the glacier.

At the next glacier a dozen seals snoozed on the packed ice flow. The crew lowered a small boat into the water and took a cameraman right up to the glacier. They were shooting a promotional video of the cruise. Near the glacier, a crewmember fished some of the glacier ice out of the ocean. When they returned, the snack bar offered complimentary drinks chilled with 100,000-year-old glacier ice. It was great!

After five hours and 26 glaciers, the catamaran headed back to Whittier. There, we caught the train and slept most of the way back to Anchorage--it was a very physical day.

On Friday July 2nd, Connie, Linda and I flew back to the lower 48 states ending a dream adventure. Karla followed a few days later. Would I do it again? *Give me five minutes to get my biking shoes on!*

REFERENCES

Alyeska Pipeline, "The Trans-Alaska Pipeline," Pipeline
    Brochure, Anchorage Alaska, June 1997.
Baker, D., "Northwest Deliveries," Aviation Magazine, July
    1943.
Basch, Marty, Against The Wind, Top of the World
    Communications, Intervale NH, 1995.
Carlson, Joe and Nancy, Joy Abounds, Wildwood Creations,
    Fairbanks AK, 1990.
Carlson, Nancy, "Alaska Homestead," Countryside Journal,
    March/April 1996.
Cohen, Stan, The Trail of '42, Missoula, Montana, 1979.
Cole, Dermot, Amazing Pipeline Stories, Epicenter Press,
    Kenmore WA, 1997.
Columbo, John R., 1001 Questions About Canada, Doubleday
    Canada, Toronto Ontario, 1986.
Curtis, Cherie, Homestead Kid, Morris Publishing, Kearney NE,
    1999.
Dziuban, Col S. W., Military Relations Between The United
    States and Canada 1939-1945, Department of the Army,
    Washington DC, 1959.
Ewing, Susan, The Great Alaskan Nature Factbook, Alaska
    Northwest Books, Anchorage Alaska, 1996.
Ford, C. and A. MacBain, "Arctic Rendezvous," Collier's
    Magazine, 12 August 1944.
Harder, Kelsie B., Illustrated Dictonnary of Place Names of
    United States and Canada, Van Nostrand Reinhold Co,
    NY NY 1976.
Hocking, Anthony, Saskatchewan, McGraw Hill Ryerson Ltd,
    Toronto Ontario, 1979.
Holloway, Sam, Collected Stories, The Yukon Magazine,
    Whitehorse Yukon, 1998.
Johnson, A.L., Ouabache Adventure--Canoeing the Wabash,
    Creative Enterprises, Dayton OH, 1991.

Johnson, A.L., Biking Across the Devil's Backbone, Creative
    Enterprises, Dayton OH, 1997.
Kakm Video, The Alaskan Highway 1942-1992, Alaska Public
    Telecommunications, Anchorage AK, 1995
London, Jack, The Call of the Wild, Penguin books, New York
    NY, 1988.
Lundberg, Murray, The Alaskan Highway, D.R. Webster
    Publishing, Whitehorse Yukon, 1999.
Maltz, Maxwell, Psycho Cybernetics, Pocket Book, NY NY,
    1960
Scully, A Collection of Trash, Truth & Trivia, Scully, Scullyville
    Yukon, 1996.
Service, Robert, The Complete Poems of Robert Service, Dodd,
    Mead & Co., NY NY 1949.
Standley, Admiral W.H., "Stalin and World Unity," Collier's
    Magazine, 30 June 1945.
Stone, Ted, Alaska & Yukon History Along The Highway, Red
    Deer College Press, Red Deer Alberta Canada, 1997.
Twichell, Heath, Northwest Epic, St. Martins Press, NY NY,
    1992.
Vergara, Valeria, "Caws and Effects – The Story of the Raven,"
    Guide to the Goldfields, Whitehorse Yukon, 1999 ed.
White, Helen editor, Alaska-Yukon Wildflower Guide, Alaska
    Northwest Books, Anchorage Alaska, 1974.
Wilson, J.A., "Northwest Passage By Air," Canadian
    Geographical Journal, March 1943.
WPA, North Dakota – A Guide to the Northern Prarie State,
    Oxford University Press, NY NY, 1950.
Zuehlke, Mark, The Yukon Fact Book, Whitecap Books,
    Vancouver British Columbia Canada, 1998.

APPENDIX 1 - ARCTIC CIRCLE BIKE ROUTE AND MILEAGE

Town	Route Out	Miles To	Cumul	Daily	Date arrival	Alt	Min/Max	Map Out	Note
Dayton	Rt 35		0		Wed 5 May	870	850-1000	Day	Wal-Mart
Eaton O	Rt 35	25	25			1000	1000-1050	Eaton	
Richmond IN	Rt 38	10	35			1050	1050-1150	Rich	
Hagerstown	Rt 38	19	54			1150	1150-1200	IN	
New Castle	Rt 38	11	65			1150	1150-1200		
Pendleton IN	Rt 38	22	87			900	900-1150		
Noblesville IN	Rt 38	16	103	103	Wed 5 May	800	800-950		Frederick-Talbott Inn - Fisher IN
Frankfort	Rt 28	39	142		Thur 6 May	900	600-900		
Attica IN	Rt 28	41	183	80	Thur 6 May	600	600-700	IN	Apple Inn - Attica IN
Illinois Line	Rt 119	18	201			700	700		IL
Potomac IL	Rt 119	16	217		Fri 7 May	700	700		
Rt 49 Armstrong	Rt 49	6	223		Fri 7 May	700	650-750		
Crescent City	Rt 49	33	256			650	650		
Kankakee IL	Rt 113	25	281	98	Fri 7 May	650	600-650		Pat's house - Minooka IL
Braidwood	Rt 113	24	305		Sat 8 May	600	600		
Rt 47	Rt 47	10	315			600	500-600		
Morris	Rt 47	6	321			500	500-600		Wal-Mart
Minooka IL	Rt 52	10	331		Sat 8 May	600	600-700		
Troy Grove	Rt 52	38	369	88	Sat 8 May	700	700-750		2 nights Pat's house - Minooka
Mendota	Rt 52	7	376		Mon 10 May	750	750-950		
Rt 30	Rt 52	20	396			800	750-800		
Dixon	Rt 52	11	407			750	650-1000		

Town	Route Out	Miles To	Cumul	Daily	Date arrival	Alt	Min/Max	Map Out	Note
Savanna IL	Rt 84	50	457	88	Mon 10 May	650	650-850		Radke Hotel - Savanna IL
Rt 20	Rt 84	19	476		Tue 11 May	850	650-1050		
Galena	Rt 84	12	488			650	650-900	IL	
Wisc Line	Rt 80	9	497			900	900-1000	WI	
Plattville WI	Rt 81	17	514			1000	1000-1100		Wal-Mart
Lancaster	Rt 35	17	531			1100	700-1100		
Bridgeport	Rt 35	28	559			700	650-700		
Prairie du Chien	Rt 35	7	566	109	Tue 11 May	650	650	WI	Holiday Motel - Prairie du Chien
La Crosse WI	Rt 14	60	626		Wed 12 May	650	650-700	WI	To La Crescent MN
Winona MN	Rt 61	40	666	100	Wed 12 May	700	700-1000	MN	Days Inn - Winona MN
Red Wing MN	Rt 61	67	733		Thur 13 May	800	800	MN	
Hastings MN	Rt 61	22	755			800	800-1000		
Rt 95	Rt 95	3	758			1000	1000		
Rt 15/5	Rt 15	15	773			1000	900-1000		
Lake Elmo MN ?		5	776	110	Thur 13 May	900	900-1000	Elmo	Mike Miller - Lake Elmo MN
I-495/Rt 55	Rt55	30	801	30	Fri 14 May	1000	1000-1100		Mike drive me across town
Buffalo MN	Rt 55	25	826			1000	1000-1200		W
Watkins	Rt 55	33	859			1200	1200-1250		
Georgeville	Rt 55	30	889			1250	1250-1400		
Glenwood MN	Rt 55	28	917	116	Fri 14 May	1250	1250-1400		Scottwood Motel -Glenwood MN
Huffman MN	Rt 55	22	939		Sat 15 May	1250	1200-1400		
Barrett MN	Rt 59	7	946			1200	1100-1250		
I-94	Rt 52	23	969			1250	1050-1300		
BarnesvilleMN	Rt 52	25	994			1050	900-1050	MN	

196

Town	Route Out	Miles To	Cumul	Daily	Date arrival	Alt	Min/Max	Map Out	Note
Fargo ND	CR 81	25	1019	102	Sat 15 May	900	900	ND	2 nights Isgrig - Fargo ND
Alton	SR 200	36	1055			900	900	ND	
Cummings	Rt 200	11	1066		Mon 17 May	900	900-1500		
Finley	Rt 200	37	1103			1500	14-1500		
Cooperstown	Rt 200	19	1122		Mon 17 May	1400	14-1500		Isgrig senior
Glenfield	Rt 200	21	1143	124	Mon 17 May	1500	15-1600		
Carrington	Rt 52	25	1168		Tue 18 May	1600	1600		
Fessenden	Rt 52	40	1208	86	Tue 18 May	1600	1600-1700		AJ's Motel - Fessenden ND
Martin	Rt 52	26	1234		Wed 19 May	1700	1700-2000		
Balfour	Rt 52	24	1258		Wed 19 May	1700	1600-1700		
Velva ND	Rt 52	21	1279		Wed 19 May	1600	1600-1700		
Minot ND	Rt 52	22	1301	93	Wed 19 May	1700	1700-2000		Sandman Motel - Minot ND
Kenmare	Rt 52	54	1355		Thur 20 May	2000	1900-2000		
Flaxton ND	Rt 52	35	1390		Thur 20 May	1900	1800-1900		
Portal ND	Rt 39	13	1403	102	Thur 20 May	1800	1800-1900	ND	Canada-Americana Motel -
Coalfield SK	Rt 39	25	1428		Fri 21 May	1800	18-1900	1	
Midale	Rt 39	27	1455		Fri 21 May	1800	18-1900	1	
Halbrite	Rt 39	9	1464		Fri 21 May	1900	1900	1	
Weyborn SK	Rt 39	19	1483	80	Fri 21 May	1900	18-1900	1/2	Circle 6 Weyburn SK
Corinne	Rt 6	45	1528		Fri 21 May	1900	1900	3	
Regina	Rt 6/11	28	1556	73	Sat 22 May	1900	18-1900		Regina InTowner Motel - Regina SK
Chamberlain	Rt 11	55	1611		Sun 23 May	1900	19-2000	3	
Davidson SK	Rt 11	37	1648	92	Sun 23 May	2000	16-2000	4	Davidson Motel - Davidson SK
Sasketoon	Rt 16/5	68	1716	68	Mon 24 May	1600	16-1700	5	Country Inn - Saskatoon SK

197

Town	Route Out	Miles To	Cumul	Daily	Date arrival	Alt	Min/Max	Map Out	Note	AK Hwy Mileage
N. Battleford	Rt 16	86	1802	86	Tue 25 May	1600	16-1900	6	Roadway Inn - N Battleford SK	
Lloydminster	Rt 16	88	1890	88	Wed 26 May	2100	16-2100	7	Imperial 400 - Lloydminster SK	
Vegreville AL	Rt 14	90	1980	90	Thur27 May	2100	21-2200	8	Vista Motel - Vegreville AB	
Edmonton	Rt 16	75	2041	75	Fri 28 May	2300	21-2500	8	Best Western City Ctr-Edmonton	
Spruce Grove	Rt 43	20	2061		Sat 29 May	2300	23-2400	8/9		
Whitecourt	Rt 43	93	2154	113	Sat 29 May	2300	23-2700	10/11	Alaskan Hwy Motel - Whitecourt	
Valleyview AL	Rt 34	106	2260	106	Sun 30 May	2200	22-2300	12	Raven Motor Inn - Valley View	
Grande Prairie	Rt 2	70	2330	70	Mon 31 May	2200	21-2200	13	Igloo Inn - Grande Prairie AB	
Beaverlodge	Rt 2	26	2356		Tue 1 Jun	2300	22-2500	13		
BC line	Rt 2	32	2388			2600	23-2600	13		
Dawson Creek	Rt 97	25	2413	83	Tue 1 Jun	2000	20-2500	14	Inn On The Creek –	0
Ft. St. John BC	Rt 97	48	2461		Wed 2 Jun	2200	20-2200	15		48
Shepherd's Inn	Rt 97	24	2485	72	Wed 2 Jun	2400	22-2400	15	Shepherd's Inn	72
Wonowon	Rt 97	29	2514		Thur 3 Jun	2800	24-2800	15		101
Pink Mountain	Rt 97	39	2553	68	Thur 3 Jun	3500	28-3500	16	PinkMountainMotorInn -	140
BuckinghorseRiver	Rt 97	31	2584		Fri 4 Jun	3500	30-3500	16		171
Prophet River	Rt 97	46	2630	77	Fri 4 Jun	2500	25-3500	17	Buckinghorse River Lodge	217
Ft. Nelson BC	Rt 97	68	2698	68	Sat 5/Sun 6 Jun	1000	10-2500	17	Travel Lodge -	285
Summit Lake	Rt 97	89	2787	89	Mon 7 Jun	4000	10-4000	18	Summit Lodge -	374
Muncho Lake	Rt 97	61	2848		Tue 8 Jun	3000	30-4000	18/19		435
Liard River	Rt 97	40	2888	101	Tue 8 Jun	2000	20-3000	20	Lower Liard Lodge	475
Coal River BC	Rt 97	36	2924		Wed 9 Jun	1500	15-2000	20		511
Fireside	Rt 97	10	2934		Wed 9 Jun	1500	1500	20		521
Iron Creek Lodge	Rt 97	39	2973	85	Wed 9 Jun	1800	15-1800	20	Iron Creek Lodge	560

Town	Route Out	Miles To	Cumul	Daily	Date arrival	Alt	Min/Max	Map Out	Note	AK Hwy Mileage
Lower Post BC Rt 1	32	3005			Thur 10 Jun	2000	15-2500	21		592
Watson Lake YK Rt 1	42	3047	74		Thur 10 Jun	2500	20-2500	22	Iron Creek Lodge	634
Upper Liard Rt 1	7	3054			Fri 11 Jun	2500	2600	22		641
Mile Marker 710 Rt1	69	3123			Fri 11 Jun	3000	25-3000	23/24/25		710
Big Creek Rec Rt 1	15	3138	91		Fri 11 Jun	2600	26-3000	22	Rancheria Motel	725
Teslin YK Rt 1	79	3217			Sat 12 Jun	2200	10-3000	26		804
Johnson's Cross Rt 1	32	3248	111		Sat 12 Jun	2200	22-3000	26	Yukon Motel	836
Rt 7 & 8 Rt 1	30	3278			Sun 13 Jun	3000	21-3000	27		866
Whitehorse YK Rt 1	51	3329	81		Sun-on 13/14 Jun	2100	20-2200	27	High Country Inn	917
Haines Junction Rt 1	99	3427	99		Tue 15 Jun	2000	7-2200	28/29	MountainViewMtrInn	1016
Silver City Rt1	35	3462			Wed 16 Jun	2500	2500	30		1051
Burwash Landing Rt1	42	3504			Wed 16 Jun	2500	25-3000	30	Burned in forest fire	1093
Kluane Lodge RT1	25	3529	102		Wed 16 Jan	2800	25-2800	30	Kluane Wilderness Ldg	1118
Koidern Rt 1	46	3575			Thur 17 Jun	3000	22-3000	30		1164
Beaver Creek Rt 1	38	3613			Thur 17 Jun	2200	22-2300	31		1202
US Border Rt 2	20	3633	104		Thur 17 Jun	2300	18-2400	AK	1202 Motor Inn	1222
Northway J AK Rt 2	42	3675			Fri 18 Jun	1800	1800-2000			1264
Tetlin Jct Rt 2	37	3712			Fri 18 Jun	1800	1800			1301
Tok AK Rt 2	12	3724	91		Fri 18 Jun	1800	1800		Young's Motel -	1313
Tanacross Rt 2	12	3736			Sat 19 Jun	1800	1800-4200			1325
Dot Lake Rt 2	36	3772			Sat 19 Jun	2400	1200-2400			1361
Delta J AK Rt 2	61	3833	109		Sat 19 Jun	1200	1000-1200		Alaska 7 Motel -	1422
Big Delta Rt 2	12	3845			Sun 19 Jun	1000	600-1400			1434
North Pole Rt 2	61	3906			Sun 20 Jun	600	600			1495

Town	Route Out	Miles To	Cumul	Daily	Date arrival	Alt	Min/Max	Map Out	Note	AK Hwy Mileage
Fairbanks	Rt2	28	3934	101	Sun/Mon 21-21 Jun	600	600-2200		Bridgewater Hotel	1523
Livengood	Dalton	75	4009	75	Tue 22 Jun	800	400-2200		Carlson's Cozy Cabins	
Yukon River	Dalton	60	4069	60	Wed 23 Jun	400	400-2200	AK	Yukon Venture Motel	
Arctic Circle	Dalton	60	4129	60	Thur 24 Jun	2000			Finish -	
Fairbanks	Dalton	195			Thur/Fri 24-25 Jun				Bridgewater Hotel	
Chena Hot Springs					Sat/Sun 26/27 Jun				Chena Hot Springs	
Healy					Mon 28 Jun				Denali North Star Inn	
Talkeetna					Tue 29 Jun				Talkeetna Roadhouse	
Anchorage					Wed/Thur 30/1 Jul				Holiday Inn	
Dayton	TWA				Fri 2 July				Fly Home	

APPENDIX 2 - MOTELS

Fredrick-Talbott Inn
13805 Allisonville Rd
Fishers IN 46038
317-578-3600 $119

Apple Inn
604 Broad St
Attica IN 47918
765-762-6574 $84

Radke Hotel
422 Main St
Savanna IL 61074
815-273-3713 $35

Holiday Inn
1010 S Marquette Rd
Prairie Du Chien WI
800-962-3883 $45

Days Inn
420 Cottonwood Dr
Winona MN 55987
507-454-6903 $50

Scottwood Motel
Hwy 55 & Hwy 28
Glenwood MN 56334
320-634-5105 $60

AJ's Motel
401 Highway 15
Fessenden ND 58438
701-547-3895 $21

Sandman Motel
2601 Burdick Expresswy W
Minot ND 58701
701-852-4088 $26

Americana Motel
18 West Railway Ave
Portal ND 58772
701-926-4991 $26

Circle 6 Motel
140Sims Ave
Weyborn SK S4H 2H5
306-842-6166 $44 Can

Intowner Motel
1009 Albert St
Regina SK S4R 2P9
306-525-3737 $45 Can

Davidson Motel
612 Railway St
Davidson SK S0G 1A0
306-567-5520 $38 Can

Country Inn
617 Cynthia St
Saskatoon SK S7L 6B7
306-934-3900 $61 Can

Roadway Inn
971 Hwy 16 Bypass
N. Battleford SK S9A 3W2
306-445-7747 $51 Can

Imperial 400
4320 44th St
Lloydminster SK S9V 1Z9
306-825-4400 $59 Can

Vista Motel
4797 50th Ave
Vegreville AB T0C 1K9
780-632-3288 $28 Can

Best Western
11310 109th St
Edmonton AB T5G 2T7
780-479-2042 $89 Can

Alaskan Highway Motel
3511 Hwy St
Whitecourt AB T7S 1N5
780-778-4156 $53 Can

Raven Motor Inn
Hwy 43 & Hwy 34
Valleyview AB T0H 3N0
780-524-3383 $ 58 Can

Igloo Inn
11724 100th st
Grande Prairie AB
780-539-5314 $56 Can

Inn On The Creek
106 W 8th St
Dawson Creek
BC V1G 3R3
250-782-8136 $44 Can

Shepherd's Inn
PO Box 6425
Ft St John BC V1J 4H8
250-827-3676 $40 Can

Pink Mountain Inn
Mile 143 Alaskan Hwy
Pink Mountain BC
V0C 2B0
250 772-3234 $55 Can

Buckinghorse River Lodge
RR 1 Box 30
Ft Nelson BC V0C 1R0
250-773-6468 $40 Can

Travel Lodge
4711 50th St
Ft Nelson BC V0C 1R0
250-774-3911 $78 Can

Summit Lodge
Mile 373 Alaskan Hwy
250-232-7531 $50 Can

Lower Liard Lodge
Box 9
Muncho Lake BC VOC 1Z0
250-776-7341 $57 Can

Iron Creek Lodge
Mile 596 Alaskan Highway
Yukon Y0A 1C0
867-536-2266 $53 Can

Rancheria Motel
Mile 710 Alaskan Highway
Yukon Y0A 1A0
867-851-6456 $60 Can

Yukon Motel
PO Box 187
Teslin Yukon Y0A 1B0
867-390-2575 $66 Can

High Country Inn
4051 4th Ave
Whitehorse YT Y1A 1H1
800-554-4471 $119 Can

Mountain View Motel
PO Box 5479
Haines Junction YT
Y0B 1L0
867-634-2646 $70 Can

Kluane Wilderness Village
Lodge
Mile 1118 Alaskan Hwy
Kluane Village YK
867-841-4141 $35 Can

1202 Motor Inn
Mile 1202 Alaskan Hwy
Beavercreek YT Y0B-1A0
867-862-7600 $150 Can

Young's Motel
PO Box 482
Tok AK 99780
907-883-4411 $ 80 US

Alaska 7 Motel
PO Box 1115
Delta Junction AK 99737
907-895-4848 $65

Bridgewater Hotel
723 First Ave
Fairbanks AK 99701
800-582-4916 $120

Carlson's Cozy Cabins
PO Box
Fairbanks AK 99701
No phone $50

Yukon Venture Motel
PO Box 60947
Fairbanks AK 99706
907-655-9001 $100

Chena Hot Springs Resort
PO Box 73440
Fairbanks AK 99707-9990
907-452-7867 $ 125

Denali North Star Inn
PO Box 240
Healy AK 99743
907-683-1560 $ 117

Talkeetna Roadhouse
PO Box 604
Talkeetna AK
907-733-1351 $ 80

Days Inn
321 East Fifth Ave
Anchorage AK 99501
907-276-7226 $139

APPENDIX 3 - ITEMS I TOOK TO ALASKA

The following are the items I carried on my bike for the trip to Alaska. Other items I needed I bought along the way, such as local guidebooks, additional maps, bike tires and additional tubes. Everything listed fit in my saddlebags, backpack, sports bag and fanny pack. The total weight of these items and bags was 35 pounds.

Clothes:
Belt — 1
Biking shorts - 1
Hankies - 4
Hat - 1
Jacket (Gortex) - 1
pants/Levies — 1
pants/long (Gortex) — 1
safety pins
sewing kit
shirt (short sleeve) — 1
shirt (long sleeve) — 1
shirt (pullover) — 1
shirt (sweat) — 1
shorts (running)— 2
sneakers - 1
socks - 3
sports carrying bag
T-shirt - 1
underwear — 3
under shirts — 3

Toiletries:
Aspirins
Bug repellent
Comb
Dental floss
First aid kit

Toiletries continued
Listerine
Iodine tablets (water)
Neosporin
Noxzema
Razor
shampoo
Shaving cream
Soap
Sun block
Talc
Toothbrush
Tooth paste
Towel – 1
vitamins
Wash cloth

Tools:
Air pump
Allen wrenches
Chain tool
Chain spare parts
Crescent wrench
Duct tape
Electrical tape
Flashlight
Fletcher tool
Knife

Tools continued
Lacing cord
Matches (waterproof)
Oil can
Screw driver
Stem adapters
Tire patch kit
Tubes — 2

Bike equipment:
Backpack
basket
bike locks — 2
bungee cords - 4
flashing/strobe-light
Gloves — 2 pair
Helmet
Hotel list
maps
rain poncho
Reflective vest
Route list
Saddlebags - 2
Shoe (bike)
Snacks
Water bottles — 2
Waterproof bags - 2
Wipe rag

Recording equipment:
Bike write-up
Book — camel
Business cards
Camera — analog
Camera — digital
Computer
Computer power converter

Recording Equip continued
Computer phone cord
Computer waterproof bag
Fanny pack
Film
Flashcard (digital camera)
Notebook — school
Notebook — pocket
Pledge forms

Personal:
Address list
Checks
Credit cards
Glasses (spare)

Food:
Granola bars
Beef jerky
Power bars

206

APPENDIX 4 – WHAT DID IT COST

The cost for my trip included buying a road bike for myself and one for my co-rider as well as mountain bikes for both of us. I purchased topographic maps for the entire route. Lodging varied from $21 to $139 a night. For the 30 days that Connie accompanied we rented two rooms. I paid the airfares for Karen, Connie and Paul to join me in Canada and our air fare back home from Alaska. Gloria shipped one road bike to Regina for Karen to ride and two mountain bikes to Edmonton for Paul and me to ride on the Alaskan Highway.

Two road bicycles	$2,350
Two mountain bicycles	1,725
Maps	425
Travel & guide books	100
Lodging (56 days)	4,210
Food (56 day)	3,400
Air Fare (Allen, Connie, Paul, Karen)	1,630
Digital camera	350
Film camera	275
Portable computer	3,310
Film and developing (30 Rolls)	270
Freight for 3 bikes to Canada	295
Van (one-way Edmonton to Anchorage)	4,080
Gas	210
Phone calls and Internet charges	900
Passports (Paul & Connie)	120
Misc. (tires, tubes, helmet, etc)	500
Total	$24,150

APPENDIX 5 - ALASKAN HIGHWAY CONDITION

Grades 10 to 1

10 = smooth asphalt with no cracks
9 = smooth asphalt with small cracks
8 = dimpled asphalt with cracks
7 = asphalt with pea gravel surface and cracks
6 = rough asphalt with loose gravel on top
5 = rough asphalt with pot holes
4 = packed gravel or dirt with pot holes
3 = chipped asphalt or loose gravel
2 = loose gravel or dirt with washboard surface
1 = dirt ruts or mud

Mile Marker	Location	Grade of Road	Width & Grade of Shoulder
0-10	Dawson Creek	9	6' - 9
10-20		8/7	4' - 8/7
20-30		8	4' - 8
30-40		8	4' - 8
40-50	Ft. St. John	8	4' - 8
50-60		8	4' - 8
60-70		8	4' - 8
70-80	Shepherd's Inn	8	4' - 8
80-90		7	4' - 7
90-100		7	4' - 7
100-110	Wonowon	6	4' - 6
110-120		6	4' - 6
120-130		6	4' - 6
130-140	Pink Mountain	5	4' - 5
140-150		5	5' - 5
150-160		5	5' - 5
160-170		5	5' - 5

Mile Marker	Location	Grade of Road	Width & Grade of Shoulder
170-180	Buckinghorse River	5	5' - 5
180-190		5	5' - 5
190-200		5	5' - 5
200-210		5	5' - 5
210-220	Prophet River	5	5' - 5
220-230		5	5' - 5
230-240		5/6	5' - 5/6
240-250		5	5' - 5
250-260		5	5' - 5
260-270		5	5' - 5
270-280		5/6	5' - 5/6
280-290	Ft. Nelson	5/6	5' - 5/6
290-300		5/6	5' - 5/6
300-310		5	6' - 5
310-320		5	3/6' - 5
320-330		5	0/3' - 4
330-340	Steamboat Mt. Lodge	5	0/3' - 4
340-350		3 gravel	0'
350-360		5	1' - 3
360-370		5	0'
370-380	Summit	5	0'
380-390		5	0'
390-400		5	gravel
400-410	Toad River Lodge	5	0'
410-420		5	0'
420-430		5	0'
430-440	Muncho Lake	5	0'
440-450		5	0'
450-460		5	0'

Mile Marker	Location	Grade of Road	Width & Grade of Shoulder
460-470		5 construction	0'
470-480	Liard River Lodge	5	0'
480-490		5	0'
490-500		5	0'
500-510		5	0'
510-520	Coal River Lodge	5	0'
520-530	Fireside	3 gravel	0'
530-540		5	6' - 5
540-550		5	6' - 5
550-560		3 gravel	0
560-570	Contact Creek Lodge	5	6' - 5
570-580	Iron Creek Lodge	5	0'
580-590		5	0'
590-600	Lower Post	3 gravel	0'
600-610		3 gravel	0'
610-620		3 gravel	0'
620-630		5	0'
630-640	Watson Lake	5	0'
640-650	Highway 37	3 gravel	0'
650-660		3 gravel	0'
660-670		5	3' - 5
670-680		5	6' - 5
680-690		4 gravel/asphalt	0'
690-700		5	6' - 5
700-710		5	6' - 5
710-720	Rancheria Motel	5	6' - 5
720-730		5	3' - 5
730-740	Swift River Lodge	5	3' - 5
740-750		5	6' - 5

Mile Marker	Location	Grade of Road	Width & Grade of Shoulder
750-760		5	6' - 5
760-770		5	3' - 5
770-780	Morley River Lodge	5	3' - 5
780-790		5	3' - 5
790-800		5	3' - 5
800-810	Teslin	5	3' - 5
810-820	Mukluk Annie's	4	3' - 3
820-830		3 gravel	0'
830-840	Johnson's Crossing	3 gravel	0'
840-850		5	3' - 5
850-860		6	3' - 6
860-870	Jake's Corner	5	3' - 4
870-880		5	3' - 4
880-890		5	3' - 4
890-900		5	3' - 4
900-910		6	3' - 4
910-920	Whitehorse	6	6' - 6
920-930	Klondike Hwy	6	6' - 6
930-940		6	6' - 6
940-950		5/4	3' - 4
950-960		5/4	3' - 4
960-970		4/3 gravel	3' - 3
970-980		5	3' - 5
980-990		5	0'
990-1000		5	0'
1000-1010		5	0'
1010-1020	Haines Junction	5	0'
1020-1030		5	0'
1030-1040		6	3' - 6

Mile Marker	Location	Grade of Road	Width & Grade of Shoulder
1040-1050		5	0'
1050-1060	Kluane Lake	5	0'
1060-1070		3 1 mile gravel	0'
1070-1080		5	0'
1080-1090	Destruction Bay	5	0'
1090-1100	Burwash Landing	5	0'
1110-1120	Kluane Wilderness Village	5	0'
1120-1130		5	0'
1130-1140	Donjek River	5/4	0'
1140-1150		5/3 gravel	0'
1150-1160		3 gravel	0'
1160-1170	White River Lodge	5	3' - 5
1170-1180		3 gravel	0'
1180-1190		3 gravel	0'
1190-1200		5/3 gravel sect	0'
1200-1210	Beavercreek	5/3 gravel	0'
1210-1220		5/3 gravel	0'
1220-1230	US/Canada border	5/3 gravel	0'
1230-1240		5	3' - 5
1240-1250		8/7	4' - 8/7
1250-1260		8/7	4' - 8/7
1260-1270	Northway Junction	5/4 some gravel	0' - 7
1270-1280	short gravel sections	7	4' - 7
1280-1290	short gravel sections	7	4' - 7
1290-1300	short gravel sections	7	4' - 7
1300-1310	Tok	8/7	4' - 8/7
1310-1320		8/7	4' - 8/7
1320-1330	Tanacross Junction	7	4' - 7
1330-1340		7/4	4' - 4

Mile Marker	Location	Grade of Road	Width & Grade of Shoulder
1340-1350		7/4	4' - 4
1350-1360		7	4' - 7
1360-1370	Dot Lake	7	4' - 7
1370-1380		7	4' - 7
1380-1390		7	4' - 7
1390-1400		3 gravel	0'
1400-1410		3 gravel	0'
1410-1420		7	3' - 7
1420-1430	Delta Junction	7/4	3' - 4
1430-1440		7	3' - 7
1440-1450		7/4 rough	3' - 7
1450-1460		7/4 gravel	3' - 3
1460-1470		7/4 gravel	3' - 3
1470-1480		7/4 gravel	3' - 3
1480-1490		7	6' - 7
1490-1500	4-lane road	7	6' - 7
1500-1510	4-lane	7	6' - 7
1510-1520	4 lane	7	6' - 7
1520-1523	Fairbanks	7	6' – 7

213

APPENDIX 6 - WILD FLOWERS

      I am indebted to our daughter-in-law, Connie, for assembling this list of wildflowers we encountered on the bike trip. Connie took the time to seek out, collect and identify over 50 beautiful wildflowers along the roadside. She carefully cataloged each new flower she found and matched it with those pictured in Helen White's Alaska-Yukon Wildflower Guide. The numbers in parentheses following the flowers are the page numbers in White's Guide where that flower appears. Connie's entheuiasum for searching for new wildflowers was sparked by her years of floral arrangement experience in a florist shop.

Alaskan Poppy, Yellow (52)
Alp Lily (10)
Alpine Arnica (179)
Arctic Larkspur (39)
Arctic Lupine
Arctic Milk Vetch (86)
Butterwart/Bog Violet (155)
Canada Goldenrod
Canadian Dwarf Dogwood (106)
Chimingbells/Languid Lady(137)
Cow Parsnip (105)
Cut Leaf Anemone (44)
Dandelion
Dodecatheon Pulchellum (4 &5)
Equisetum Fluvatile
Equisetum Sylvaticum
Fairyslippers (25)
Fireweed (50)
Giant Ostrich Ferns
Goatsbeard (71)
Golden Corydalis (53)
Lagotis/Weasel Snout (143)
Lapland Diapensia (120)
Marsh Marigold (37)
Mastodon/Marsh Fleabane (180)
Monkshood (40)

Mountain Harebell
Mountain Marigold (42)
Mountain Sorrel
Narcissus – Flowered (43)
Nodding or Bulblet Saxifrage(67)
Nootha Lupine (85)
Northern Anemone (42)
Northern Bedstraw (156)
Northern Jasmine
Northern Yellow Oxytrope (91)
Pasque Flower/Wild Crocus (45)
Pink Poppy (49)
Prickly Wold Rose (85)
Saxifraga, Red Stemmed 118/119
Silver Weed (78)
Strawberry Blite (30)
Sundew, Long Leaved (57)
Tall Jacob's Ladder (133)
Thyme – Leaved Saxifrage (76)
Tufted White Cotton Grass (7)
Two Flowered Cinquefoil (76)
Walpole Poppy (48)
Western Columbine (38)
White Bog Orchid (19)
Wild Iris, Blue Flag
Wild Sweet Pea (92)

INDEX

Books By Allen Johnson

[ ]   BIKING TO THE ARCTIC CIRCLE

"Bike to the Arctic Circle? Impossible! There's ice and snow up there," my friend said. Regardless, I did cycle to the Arctic Circle.

As a child I dreamed of traveling the Alaskan Highway. When I started planning the trip our grandson agreed to bike the 1,000 mile Alaskan Highway portion. My office-mate rode the first 800 miles, our niece cycled across Canada and my neighbor rode the Alaskan portion.

Jim and I started from Dayton in May 1999. The first day I had three flat tires, broke a spoke and bent my wheel so bad it wouldn't rotate. I wondered if the Lord was telling me the ride was a dumb idea.

The prettiest part of our lower-48-state ride was biking along the Mississippi River's Great River Road from Savanna IL to Minneapolis MN. Bald eagles soaring overhead, deer peeking out of the wooded hills and tugboats pushing barges up river.

Karen joined me in Regina SK and rode one week. We fought head winds across Sask., pedaling 14 hours one day to go 85 miles. The next day we covered the same distance in 6 hours with a tail wind. In Vegreville, AB we encountered a 5,000 pound Ukrainian Easter Egg.

Grandson Paul joined me in Edmonton AB. A few days later we biked into Dawson Creek, BC where the Alaskan Highway starts. Along the Alaskan Highway we encountered moose, deer, caribou, elk, buffalo, mountain sheep, wolves, black bear, grizzly bears, fox, lynx, coyotes, beaver, hares, porcupines, weasels, swans, eagles and owls.

At Whitehorse, Yukon Karla joined me and biked the final leg of the trip. In Fairbanks I switched to a mountain bike for the 200-miles of gravel road to the Arctic Circle. We spent the next night in Joy AK with the Carlsons who raised 23 children in a log cabin with no electricity, running water or indoor toilet.

On 24 June 1999 I biked across the Arctic Circle line, completing the 4,081-mile ride in 51 days. Worth the effort? You bet!   **$15.00**

[ ] AUSTRALIA FROM THE BACK OF A CAMEL

The 12 camels plodded through Rainbow Valley in the Australian outback. Kelsey, the author's 7-year-old granddaughter, nudged her 1,000-pound camel in the belly and Charcoal charged off in a cloud of dust, galloping to the head of the line. The author and 3 of his grandchildren were on a 7-day camel safari in the middle of the Australian desert. They spent 8 hours a day riding camels in search of caves with Aboriginal paintings, fossils, desert animals and unusual flora and fauna. At night, the Johnsons slept on the ground around a huge fire to ward of the near-freezing temperature. It was winter in the desert, with daytime temperatures of 80 to 90F, but at night it dropped to 30 degrees F. They encountered wallabies, kangaroos, wedge-tailed eagles, dingos, emus and a variety of desert birds, lizards, snakes and spiders. The Johnsons sampled the desert foods, including eating a three-inch long witchery grub. The best part of the trip: "Running the camels across the dry lake-bed," Kelsey said. "Seeing how my grandchildren handled new situations," was Allen's reply. **$16.95**

[ ] BIKING ACROSS THE DEVIL'S BACKBONE

A 9-year-old and her grandfather pedaled 600 miles across the mid-West in search of adventure. Enroute they explored Cave-in-Rock on the Ohio River, the Garden of the Gods in southern Illinois, visited an ostrich farm in Mt. Vernon, spent the night with the monks at St. Meinrad Monastery, toured Lincoln's boyhood home in southern Indiana and pedaled over the razorback Devil's Backbone. Tracy maintained her good humor and high spirits while pedaling up to 65 miles a day through the hilly route in 95-degree heat. The best part of the trip? "The day at the monastery," replied Tracy. "Spending time with my granddaughter," explained Allen. **$15.95**

[ ] CANOEING THE WABASH

An adventure-packed 500-mile long trip canoeing down the Wabash River with the author and his 10-year-old grandson. From Fort Recovery, Ohio, they dragged the canoe through the shallow, upper Wabash, fought raging rapids and survived a 14-hour long thunder-lightening storm. At night the pair camped and fished along the banks of the river. They encountered deer, raccoons, muskrats, rabbits, beaver, gars and pileated woodpeckers during their 16-day journey along the still-wild river. The trip was a physical challenge and an educational experience. Along the river they visited Ft. Recovery, Tippecanoe Battlegrounds and the George Rogers Clark monument.

After paddling one-quarter-million strokes they finally reached their destination--the Ohio River. The author weaves a tale of adventure, history and humor into a delightful package.   **$13.95**

[ ]   DRIVE THROUGH RUSSIA? IMPOSSIBLE!

In 1981, the author and his wife rented a car and drove 4,000 miles through the Communist Soviet Union by themselves. This book describes the 3-week odyssey through the ancient countryside and modern bureaucracy. When the Johnsons first entered the Soviet Union, the officials informed them they would be staying the in the Pribaltiskaya Hotel that night in Leningrad. "What is the name of our hotel in Novgorod tomorrow night?" Allen asked. "It is not necessary for you to know. Tomorrow we will tell you where you will be staying." The author found that in the Soviet Union, information was power and the officials were very reluctant to give it away. With a basic understanding of the Russian language learned from 3 years of tutoring in Dayton before the trip, the Johnsons traveled from town to town, purchased food and gasoline, interpreted the meager road maps and visited with the Russian people. They found the people curious, kind and helpful. Travel with the Johnsons and enjoy a vivid picture of their daily discoveries, pleasures and frustrations.   **$10.95**

Order With This Convenient Coupon

Creative Enterprises
1040 Harvard Blvd.
Dayton OH 45406-5047

Please send me the books I have checked above. I am enclosing $_____ (please add $2.00 per book for postage/handling. Ohio residents add 6.5% tax). Send check or money order. You can also order from the Internet: **http://www.creative-enterprises.org or toll free from 888-BOOKS77.**

Name_____

Address_____

City_____ State _____ Zip Code _____

Allow 2--4 weeks for delivery.